jump into the

JACUZZI

Published by
The Bible Reading Fellowship
Sandy Lane West, Oxford, England
ISBN 0 7459 3251 7

First edition 1998
10 9 8 7 6 5 4 3 2 1 0

Acknowledgments
p.11 Extract from 'Emerging' from *Collected Poems 1945–1990* by
R.S. Thomas, published by J.M. Dent.
p.24 Extract from 'Heaven Shall Not Wait' (Wild Goose
Publications, 1987), words by John L. Bell & Graham Maule, copyright © 1987 WGRG, Iona Community, 840 Govan Road, Glasgow
G51 3UU, Scotland. Reproduced by permission.
pp.25, 84 Collects from Morning Prayer from *The Alternative
Service Book 1980* are copyright © The Central Board of Finance of
the Church of England and are reproduced by permission.
pp.26 Extracts from *Holy Sonnets of the 20th Century* by D.A.
Carson, published by Crossway Books Ltd, 1994, used by permission.
pp.31 Extracts from 'East Coker' from *Collected Poems 1909–1962*
by T.S. Eliot, used by permission of Faber & Faber Ltd.
p.55 Extract from *Youth A Part* (Church House Publishing, 1996)
is copyright © The Central Board of Finance of the Church of
England and is reproduced by permission.
p.70 Extract from *The Name of the Rose* by Umberto Eco, published by Martin Secker & Warburg, 1983, used by permission.
p.81 Extract taken from the song 'From heaven you came, helpless
babe' by Graham Kendrick, copyright © 1983 Kingsway's
Thankyou Music, PO Box 75, Eastbourne, East Sussex, BN23
6NW, UK. Used by permission.
Unless otherwise stated, scripture quotations are taken from the
Good News Bible published by The Bible Societies/HarperCollins
Publishers Ltd UK © American Bible Society 1966, 1971, 1976, 1992.

A catalogue record for this book is available
from the British Library

Printed and bound in Malta
by Interprint Ltd.

thirstQuenchers

jump into the

JACUZZI

Simon Heathfield

Contents

Introduction

By the reading of scripture I am so renewed that all nature seems renewed around me and with me. The sky seems to be a pure, a cooler blue, the trees a deeper green, light is sharper on the outlines of the forest and the hills and the whole earth is charged with the glory of God and I feel fire and music in the earth under my feet.

Thomas Merton, *The Sign of Jonas*

Egg foo yung, Saturday afternoon football, the slow movement of Mahler's fifth symphony, a long, deep, slow bath, parachuting, the smell of wet grass, Street Fighter 3, Elton John, a walk in the country, Magnum ice-creams, DIY projects, early Genesis albums, English puddings. What is it that you are passionate about? What gets you really excited? I'm sorry if your favourite is not in the list above; do feel free to add it in now. In fact, spend a few moments remembering the feelings, sounds, sights, smells, and emotions that accompany your favourite things...

Welcome back! Keep those memories in mind as you read on. In life we have some things about which we are passionate, often because they renew and excite our own passions. However, egg foo yung, or anything else for that matter, soon fades into the background when compared with the thrill, excitement and satisfaction of working in partnership with the living God. *Jump into the Jacuzzi* aims to refresh and renew that vision, passion and focus. To enter into that experience all we need do is to look into, and learn from, the Bible, from which God promises to speak, refreshing our minds, souls and bodies. In that process we come to know that the 'whole earth is charged with the glory of God' and begin to 'feel fire and music in the earth under our feet'.

So *Jump into the Jacuzzi* is about discovering excitement, vision and passion from the scriptures concerning the possibilities of working with children or young people. It aims to encourage you to 'jump into' those scriptures in a variety of different ways, helping you to understand and experience what God will say to you through them.

It is a distinct resource because:
• *it is not primarily a 'How to...' book on youth or children's ministry, although* **it contains practical pointers and advice;**
• *it is not primarily for either youth or children's leaders, but* **it is equally for anyone working with either children or young people, or both;**
• *it is not primarily for the children or young people, but* **they will benefit enormously as leaders are renewed and refreshed;**
• *it is not primarily for one sort of person, because* **it uses a variety of different learning styles and activities to suit a wide range of people.**

There is a misconception about ministry with children or young people that it is dependent upon certain skills and abilities: playing football, wearing trendy clothes, liking the current top band, enjoying clearing up sick, or being able to teach. These things are important and all leaders should aim to grow and develop their gifts and skills, but they are not necessarily of first importance. After some years in practical ministry, and having been privileged to watch others of greater maturity and experience, I am convinced that work with children and young people is primarily concerned with something more important than just skills. It seems to me that we are called into an activity of **active imagination**. That may sound a bit 'airy-fairy', so let me try to explain! We are called in ministry to try to discern what God is doing, and to see some of the possibilities of that activity. The way we begin to join in those possibilities is by reflecting on what we do with God's revelation of his ways, plans and purposes in the Bible. There is encouragement that we will be on the right track because, as Paul told Timothy, the Bible has its source in God (2 Timothy 3:16–17), through people, and shows us who God is and how we can live in right relationship with him and his world.

Our use of scripture is perhaps best thought of as a conversation with God where we ask questions of the text and, in turn, expect the text to ask questions of us. Through such a conversation we can begin to go beyond the literal meaning of the words. The scriptures then become *a way of seeing, of revelation*: a window revealing a wider view; a telescope bringing the far-off near, a port-hole through which to comprehend the storm; a microscope revealing the detail; a pair of spectacles correcting our perceptions. Sometimes the glass will be crystal clear; at other times fogged up and difficult to see through.

However, incredibly, as we enter into that process we begin to find that what we thought impossible is actually possible with God. As we actively begin to imagine, and see what God could do, we are constantly surprised by what God does do! So our imagining begins to shape our activity, and our activity drives yet more imagination. Just in case you are worried, thinking that you have the imagination of a small frozen pea, don't worry! As we take in more of what God says in the scriptures, we begin to find that God works through us, uniting and shaping our thoughts with his joyful creativity, bringing change and refreshment to all our life. We are drawn into God's activity, a God who says, 'I am telling you the truth: whoever believes in me will do what I do—yes, they will do even greater things, because I am going to the Father.' (John 14:12) So anyone who believes can be called into this activity, and that includes you and me!

This is much more than just skills and abilities. It is about actively imagining in

wonder—wonder of both the creator and the creation, because Christian ministry is a life-affirming activity. It is about actively imagining **redemption**—redemption for God's whole creation through Jesus Christ, because Christian ministry looks for, and towards, redemption. It is about actively imagining **hope**—hope for a future with God that is both here and now, and also certainty for the future, because Christian ministry is a hope-giving activity.

In *Jump into the Jacuzzi* there is material for the tired, the interested, the passionate, the intrigued, and many more, all of whom can be refreshed and renewed by such a vision—God's vision of ministry with him.

How does *Jump into the Jacuzzi* fit together?

Jump into the Jacuzzi is split into twelve major sections, each called an *Oasis*, and each with a particular theme, covering a wide range of issues related to youth or children's ministry. It is not the last word on youth or children's ministry and there are many important practical issues that are covered in other resources. However, it does focus on the principles and vision for ministry, which are so vital to dynamic and refreshing work. The first three *Oases* focus on the leader's relationship with God, past, present and future. The second three look at some of the skills and issues involved in working with children or young people. The third group considers the context in which ministry takes place: the leadership team, the local church and the wider society. The final three *Oases* look at some of the tensions in ministry, between giving and receiving, between leadership and service, and between ministry and home life.

Within each *Oasis* there are the following sections:
Plugging In, *which introduces the theme and materials for the Oasis as a whole.*
Testing the Water, *six sections of written material, and thought-provoking*

quotations, to help you start thinking about some Bible passages that deal with the issues under consideration.

***Taking the Plunge**, six sets of two or three questions related to the material in 'Testing the Water'. These will help you understand the passage further and give some ideas for applying it to your situation.*

***Soaking In**, a meditation on a theme, or Bible passage, from the topic of the Oasis. These aim to provide a way of thinking creatively about the material in the Oasis, particularly for those who prefer an approach other than text or questions.*

***Overflow**, an exercise for individuals to apply a theme or passage from the Oasis to practical ministry.*

***Flooded Out!** an exercise for leadership teams to do together to apply the material in the rest of the Oasis and develop their ministry.*

What sort of person is *Jump into the Jacuzzi* for?

Jump into the Jacuzzi incorporates a wide variety of approaches to thinking, praying and imagining. There is no set order to work through the book, so you can start wherever you like. Where you start will depend on the sort of person you are. If you like practical activities, you might begin with something from the 'Soaking In', 'Overflow' or 'Flooded Out!' sections before having a look at 'Testing the Water' or 'Taking the Plunge'. If you are primarily a thinker, you might want to start with 'Taking the Plunge', form your own ideas, and then look at the other sections. If you like to be stimulated first, then you might start with the 'Testing the Water' sections before moving on. So there should be something for everyone. However, remember, wherever you start, always to be ready to try something different. It is often surprising to see what helps you to grow and develop as a leader.

It is important to understand that, as well as different types of people, *Jump into the Jacuzzi* has been written with different types of work in mind. The common component is that all the ministry envisaged is Christian! But beyond that, because it concentrates on biblical principles and vision rather than specific models, you could be involved in almost any style of ministry, and still find something useful.

How can I use *Jump into the Jacuzzi*?

As you will have gathered by now, *Jump into the Jacuzzi* provides a variety of ways to explore some biblical principles for youth or children's ministry. It has been written to allow you to 'pick and mix' material according to your own preferences and needs. So use it in any way that suits you, to train, refresh, encourage and develop your ministry, but here are three ideas to get you started.

1. **Time out with God for personal refreshment and development.** If you already use an existing 'quiet time' resource, or have a pattern of daily time with God, you could use *Jump into the Jacuzzi* to provide a different focus for those times—perhaps when your group is not meeting, or simply as a change. There are six short passages in each 'Testing the Water' section, which could be used for six days of a week, or over two weeks, for a ten-minute time with God. If you have more time, you could also use some of the questions in 'Taking the Plunge'. Try to make some extra time each week to look at one of the practical activities. If you do not regularly have time aside with God each day, why not use *Jump into the Jacuzzi* to try it out? Don't try to do too much at once; try a week or two to start with and aim to find the right time of day.

2. **A training or encouragement course for those involved in youth or children's ministry.** Although it is good to

make use of specialist trainers from outside agencies, remember that by using *Jump into the Jacuzzi* you can help to develop yourself and those with whom you work. After all, you are the experts on your groups and your area! If you are unsure where to start, choose one *Oasis* from each section (try 1, 4, 7 and 10, for a four-evening course). If you know your training needs, then just pick material to suit. The week before each training evening, ask people to read as many passages from the relevant 'Testing the Water' section as possible. This will mean the precious time you have together will be really useful. When you meet you could use a mixture of the questions from 'Taking the Plunge', and the practical activities in 'Soaking In', 'Overflow' and 'Flooded Out!' It is helpful if each session has a discussion element to allow people to talk about what they have been thinking, an activity element to build upon that and a praying element to 'pray in' the lessons learnt. Try to give a third of the time to each. If you are not used to leading 'training' sessions remember to try to:

• *give people something to read or do beforehand that will prepare them to contribute during the session;*
• *stick to the time limit;*
• *encourage everyone to contribute— don't allow one person to dominate;*
• *be specific and focused, but avoid 'red herrings';*
• *value new and unusual ideas;*
• *help each person to identify one action that they need to take within twenty-four hours of the meeting.*

3. **To make encouragement and refreshment a regular part of your ministry.** If you work with others, make sure you meet regularly to plan and pray for your work. If you work alone, find someone in the church who is interested in supporting you; it might be your minister but could be anyone willing to be committed to you. Pick a suitable *Oasis* and select one item from 'Testing the Water'

and one of either 'Soaking In', 'Overflow' or 'Flooded Out!' Do the material from 'Testing the Water' before your meeting and use the other item as one element of your planning meeting. Make sure you do this every time you meet, to ensure your team is constantly encouraged and refreshed.

You might also use *Jump into the Jacuzzi* as:
• *material for a leaders' 'reading week';*
• *the focus for a relaxing weekend away for youth and children's leaders and their families;*
• *a way of structuring your own 'quiet day' or 'quiet evening';*
• *ideas for a 'just looking' evening for prospective leaders or helpers;*
• *study material for church home or study groups to think about work with children and young people.*

As you can see, *Jump into the Jacuzzi* is a very flexible resource. There are as many ways of using it as there are different styles of team and work. Make use of your imagination and see what happens!

However you choose to use *Jump into the Jacuzzi*, remember that it aims to refresh and envision those involved in or supporting Christian work with children and young people. It does not tell you everything you need to know and will not answer all your questions, and it will even leave you with some decidedly loose ends. But don't worry, those will help you to keep thinking and praying things through. Whatever you choose, remember that the focus should always be on God. Come to him expecting that he will speak, and aim to obey what he says. If you ensure such a focus you will discover the incredible refreshment and renewal that is in store for anyone who jumps into God's word, the Bible. Enjoy the trickles, the rivers, the downpours and the floods of God as he fills your active imagination with wonder, redemption and hope. And as you are refreshed and enabled to minister in his name, may his glory be seen in all you do.

OASIS I

Plugging In ...

Where does it begin?

'Oh no!' you cry. 'Not again.'

Tim has just decided to hit Reza. After all, the story is Joshua and the walls of Jericho, and to a normal five-year-old it seemed the most natural thing in the world to do, especially when, as Tim is at pains to point out, you did say, 'Let's act it out, so that we can understand the story more fully.' Unfortunately, Tim always seems to be acting it out. The rest of the session takes a nose-dive: a broken window, paint on the new carpet, and three of the smaller girls who decide that this morning is their moment to burst spontaneously into tears. (Tim was elsewhere discussing the ethics of Rahab's lifestyle with a rather shocked Sally.) By 11.45, after the vicar's sermonathon ('inspired by the Spirit'), you are desperate to escape. It crosses your mind to ask the vicar if the Holy Spirit owns a watch, but your thoughts evaporate into a haze of pure bliss as you see parents standing in the doorway. Exhausted again, your mind wanders over the questions that seem to come with increasing regularity: what am I doing this for? Surely other leaders don't have these problems? There must be something I can do! Perhaps I should just give up...?

Those working with children or young people might sympathize with the situation described above. The names, places and situation may be different, but many know the feeling. There are times when it seems the most important job in the world, and yet, both the work and the worker can easily become a physical, emotional and spiritual desert—in the words of the psalmist, a 'dry, worn out and waterless land' (Psalm 63:1). Many long for refreshment, physical, emotional and spiritual. In this first *Oasis* we will go for a paddle in Genesis, 1 Corinthians 3 and Psalm 107 to discover how and where refreshment may be found. The focus will be firmly on God and his nature, seeing how it affects who we are and what we do. So don't be shy, get your togs on, test the water and take the plunge wherever it suits you. Soak it up and experience God changing you and overflowing into your life and the lives of those whom you serve!

✳ Eternal God   Psalm 107:1–3

Give thanks to the Lord, because he is good; his love is eternal! (Psalm 107:1)

For everything that is depends on Him-who-is.

Gregory of Nyssa, *Catechetical Oration 25*

Perhaps one of the most awe-inspiring Christian concepts is that God is eternal. As finite, time-dominated (particularly in the West!) creatures, it is hard for us to understand an infinite God who stands outside of time. Gregory of Nyssa, writing in the early years of Christianity, saw the infinite nature of God reflected through and in his creation. This God was 'in the beginning', and it is his nature to create, to bring order from chaos, a characteristic that is reflected in all his dealings with creation.

As 'Him-who-is' continues to interact with 'everything that is', another astounding fact is shown: that his attitude to his creation is one of steadfast love. Probably written in response to the return from exile ('brought you back from foreign countries'), Psalm 107 calls on all of God's people to proclaim this steadfast love. Into the desolating experience of exile the eternal God speaks, offering return and restoration from the darkest period in Israel's history. Amidst changing, busy lives and pressured ministry, allow these facts to soak into the core of your being:

- *God is the eternal 'Him-who-is'; he is creator and sustainer;*
- *God's loving purposes are steadfast and faithful, reaching into the darkest of situations.*

✳ Saving God   Psalm 107:4–7

They were hungry and thirsty and had given up all hope. Then in their trouble they called to the Lord, and he saved them from their distress. He led them by a straight road to a city where they could live. (Psalm 107:5–7)

For there is no despair so absolute as that which comes with the first moments of our first great sorrow, when we have not yet known what it is to have suffered and be healed, to have despaired and to have recovered hope.

George Eliot, *Adam Bede*

It is hard for us to imagine what it was like for Israel plunged into exile. To 'wander in the trackless desert' and not be able to find their way to a city. From the time of Abraham onwards, God's promises for his people were bound up in the provision of a land where they could live and serve him. All that the nation held dear—the temple, royal family, palace, and Jerusalem itself—was either destroyed or deported. in the events of 586BC. This great sorrow and despair in the national life of Israel became its defining experience.

Eliot's apt description of absolute despair is mirrored in

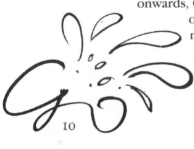

Psalm 107. The eternal, loving God seemed to have forsaken his people. Imagine then the reaction as Israel is reinstated to the land, some fifty years later: somehow the eternal God has been vindicated. Not only has there been refreshment from God, but also restoration by God. Suffering and despair have given way to healing and hope.

For us who stand on the other side of Jesus' life and ministry, we can see this action of God on an even bigger stage.

All who wander, thirsty in the desert of sin-filled lives without God, can now find the water that will mean they will never thirst again and are reinstated to a city in which the glory of God shines (Revelation 21:22–27). The eternal God continues to offer restoration and satisfaction. The experience of exile and alienation, physical, emotional or spiritual, confronts us and those we serve, each and every day. The way out for all is found in our willingness to be led by, and be vulnerable to, Him-who-is.

✴ Active God   Psalm 107:8–9

They must thank the Lord for his constant love, for the wonderful things he did for them. He satisfies those who are thirsty... (Psalm 107:8–9)

> *We are beginning to see*
> *now it is matter is the scaffolding*
> *of spirit... so in everyday life*
> *it is the plain facts and natural happenings*
> *that conceal God and reveal him to us*
> *little by little under the mind's tooling.*
>
> R.S. Thomas, *Emerging*

The exiled people of God gave thanks; they took pleasure in their restoration from exile. But what would the untutored eye, the 'untooled' mind, have seen? A distant event that we can only just describe? The rise of the Persian kingdom, a product of historical chance? Yet in these events we see a God who is in the business of revelation. An eternal, loving, redeeming and revealing God.

Earlier in my life I trained as a musician. As I advanced, I learned to see beyond the notes and begin to read something of the intent and sense of the composer. So Christian people are called to see, in the 'scaffolding' of everyday events, the Spirit of the eternal God at work. And so giving thanks is not glib or trite, defying the real awfulness of the world. Rather, it is an exercise in second sight, allowing us to reorientate our lives. We become less dependent on good feelings or worldly 'success' as we begin to see God's revelation as the centre of history, and ourselves as living in a kingdom which is both visible yet also hidden. And as we change our way of seeing, we begin to value both the creator and his creation in a new way, entering the delight of God himself, and discovering the true nature of thankfulness. Philip

Toynbee began to appreciate this second sight as his terminal cancer progressed, writing one month before his death:
Wet leaves of may and sycamore after a heavy shower... such things I look at with renewed intensity and happiness—

not because I may not see them for much longer, but because they are of immediate significance: almost direct manifestations of heavenly light.
(Philip Toynbee, End of a Journey)

✴ Second sight 1 Corinthians 3:5

After all, who is Apollos? And who is Paul? We are simply God's servants, by whom you were led to believe. Each one of us does the work which the Lord gave him to do. (1 Corinthians 3:5)

But if I, even for a moment, accept my culture's definition of me, I am rendered harmless. I can denounce evil and stupidity all I wish and will be tolerated in my denunciations as a court jester is tolerated.

Eugene H. Peterson, *The Gift*

Second sight also applies to the ministry in which we are involved. In one of the most cosmopolitan, sex-obsessed, hedonistic cities and cultures of his day, Paul struggled against the party spirit and division of the Corinthian church. Non-Christian thinking had infiltrated the church: 'You don't want to do it like that,' people said. 'Forget Paul. I follow Apollos, now there's a real apostle!' C.K. Barrett suggests that people 'wished to be at the centre of, and to control, their own religion, and had not yet learned what it meant to walk by faith, not by sight.' That second sight—faith— would have led them to the right attitude: that any Christian minister or ministry primarily belongs to, and is used by, the eternal God himself.

The incredible fact of Christian ministry is that you and I are caught up in the continuation of God's creating and redeeming work, which only he can bring to fruition. We are privileged to walk alongside God, and not simply be passive observers, but rather valued friends entrusted with responsibility. We are God's servants. But often we actually believe what human people, Christian and non-Christian, believe about Christian work with children and young people: 'Thanks for looking after (i.e. baby-sitting) the kids'; 'Isn't it good that the church gives young people something to do.' The effect can be fatal: the work becomes mere entertainment, and the worker becomes stagnant as the flow of life-giving water is stopped. All that's left to do, as Peterson suggests, is buy pointy hats with bells on! But actually, being God's servant, doing his work, is the most powerful and subversive activity in which it is possible to be involved. For we serve the eternal creator God who has a track record of subverting situations to bring about refreshment and restoration: creation from chaos, return from exile, life from death.

✳ Jealousy   1 Corinthians 3:6–9a

The one who sows and the one who waters really do not matter. It is God who matters, because he makes the plant grow. (1 Corinthians 3:7)

There is a sort of jealousy which needs very little fire; it is hardly a passion but a blight bred in the cloudy, damp despondency of uneasy egoism.

George Eliot, *Middlemarch*

Families have skeletons in the cupboard, professions have unspoken failures, and almost all ministry has taboos that we are afraid to name. Rivalry and jealousy are taboos to be found; so obvious from our personality-centred publicity, petty arguments or daggered looks. But they are unnamed, almost as if as long as we claim we cannot see them, they will be unable to affect us. But Paul gets to the central issue: we are all servants serving God equally. We have different jobs, but none is more important than another. The one who is skilled at talking to teenagers on the street is as important as the helper in the under-fives' group; they serve the same God. Any greater status or value that we see in different tasks is an illusion, born of the mistake of accepting what the world says about ministry. Much good Christian work with children and young people flounders on jealousy born of the 'damp despondency of uneasy egoism'. We need to look back to God and discover that it is he who matters, because 'he makes the plant to grow'. We are partners, bound to each other, working under his direction. Take note in these verses that Paul is not suggesting bland conformity; Apollos and Paul clearly had distinctive gifts and personalities. But as we begin to see that all are valuable in God's sight, refreshment from God comes through each of us being what he intended. Jealousy is rejected, as we no longer need such destructive crutches for our fragile egos. Refreshment is given and shared as we discover God in, and through, each other.

✳ Back at the centre   1 Corinthians 3:5–11

For God has already placed Jesus Christ as the one and only foundation, and no other foundation can be laid. (1 Corinthians 3:11)

God weeps with us so that someday we might laugh with him.

Jurgen Moltmann, *The Way of Jesus Christ*

This *Oasis* started by focusing back on God. We saw that renewal comes when we accept that God is creator, sustainer, and restorer, to name but a few. Continuing his attack on party divisions, Paul suggests that he is an 'expert builder', literally an architect, whose work can only have meaning because of the work of others: carpenters, bricklayers etc. But then he narrows the argument even further. We do not only work aware of God as some great other who controls history, but we also build on the foundation, Jesus Christ. So the eternal God who works through us is not unknown, but is personally revealed in Jesus. The only foundation upon which we can build is Jesus himself, made possible because of his death and resurrection. Amidst a weekly need to teach others about Jesus many leaders allow their foundations to shift and end up building on their own experience and knowledge. In time this becomes a dry event in the distant past rather than a present, living relationship. Such foundations are weak and may ultimately fail both ourselves and those we serve. Building that lasts requires different foundations. Our foundation, Jesus Christ, is not simply trapped in the historical situation of his life and death, but is alive now, risen and ascended with the Father. He is not distant or inactive but, as Paul reminded the Romans, is one of us who is 'at the right hand of God [and] intercedes for us' (Romans 8:34). True refreshment and restoration is to be found in the one who 'satisfies those who are thirsty and fills the hungry with good things'. That requires living water and the bread of life. Not the Jesus of the Christmas card or moral teacher, but the living Jesus, the living God, who weeps with you and me in the reality of life, so that we will laugh and rejoice with him, now and ever more.

Taking the Plunge

1. Read Psalm 107, verses 4–7. Why did God 'lead them by a straight road'? If God appears not to do this, how does it affect us? When in your life have you known the eternal God, and how do you appreciate his steadfast love?
2. What might it have been like to experience the exile? (Read Psalm 137 to start you thinking.) Have you ever felt like God has left you? Who moved, you or him?
3. Since you have been a Christian how have you begun to see God, and the world, in a different light? In your work with children and young people where, or in whom, do you find it hardest to see God at work?
4. How do you really view your ministry: life-changing or mind-numbing? What might your church, minister, children and young people have to say about it? Where in your life and ministry does God need to be subversive and bring about refreshment and restoration?
5. What relationships in your life and ministry have been damaged by jealousy, and need restoration? What might your role be in that process? What gifts has God given you for building?
6. In what ways do you build up your own Christian life? What one change could you make to help this? How might you enable those whom you serve to do the same?

Soaking In

Make some time during the week for yourself and God to 'chew over' a verse from the passages in this *Oasis*. This is not simply an exercise in thinking, it is one of imagination and exploration. A good passage to take might be Psalm 107 verses 8–9.

You will need to find a comfortable space where you will not be disturbed for at least 15 minutes. If you have children and/or a busy schedule this can be difficult, but it's worth making a priority. If you have a spouse, find a point when they can cover the phone, or take the kids out for a while. It's worth it!

Start with a short prayer asking God's Holy Spirit to teach, refresh and challenge. As you sit, begin to mull the verses over in your mind, perhaps by saying them slowly five times, letting the words sink in. Begin to ask yourself simple, direct questions: how does it feel to be really thirsty or hungry? What is it like to be refreshed or filled? Ask questions that come to mind about each part of the verse and begin to focus in on one idea. You may find it helpful to fast on the day that you choose to do this (be aware of any personal medical implications, and remember to drink). Ask yourself what God is saying through the scriptures to your life now? What are the points of contact, encouragement or tension?

If you are easily distracted, keep a pad and pen by you and write down anything that comes into your head. Then you can forget it; it will still be there later.

Overflow

Go for a walk round the area from which your children and young people come. If you are in a large gathered church then use a map, road atlas or globe, whichever is more suitable! (If all else fails, use a list of names.) As you pass by houses, schools or places, think of the individuals that come to mind and ask God to show you what he is doing in their lives and how you can serve him in that relationship. You may want to do it with someone else and share your thoughts when you return.

Flooded Out!

Arrange a meeting for leaders of as many different age groups as possible (if you are the only one, meet with your vicar and/or interested parents) and agree that you will not talk any business at all. Suggest that people read 'Testing the Water'— 'Active God' and 'Second sight' on pages 11–12 sometime before the meeting. Arrange some really good refreshments that you know suit your group. When you get together, give thanks for the food, enjoy eating and talk to each other about what good things God has been doing in your groups. Encourage each other to see God working in the ordinary, the child who is able to stay in the group, a stronger relationship with that difficult teenager… whatever! Set aside the last 20 minutes to pray. You might use these words together, encouraging people to say short prayers naming things before God:

Individual: Lord we thank you for… Our Father God,
All: **Thank you, Lord!**

ＯASIS 2

Plugging In...

Comings and goings

Four days to go before you can get home. The children's camp is going really well, the eight and nine-year-olds are having a great time, and you're just beginning to enjoy your leadership role. Heading up the teaching programme has brought both new challenges and much satisfaction. However, as the main evening meeting starts, your heart sinks as you realize that the person leading has little or no self-awareness. Inappropriate words, exaggerated actions, lack of eye contact, and awkward presence could all be the result of nervousness, but as the event progresses you realize that they signify much more. It seemed such a good idea to use the meetings as a time when people could learn and practise new skills. But this was more than you had bargained for. As you wonder what you will say in the feedback session, your mind wanders back to when you were starting out in ministry, and to those who gave you the space to make mistakes.

How well do you know yourself? Not only your likes and dislikes but the way you think, what excites you, how you react to others, your physical, emotional and spiritual background, needs and preferences? All these things form the context within which our faith and ministry operate, but they also need to be challenged and changed as we understand and grow in our faith. The call of faith is a call to change towards what God created us for; life with him for eternity. So as we exercise Christian ministry we are encouraging and encountering change in ourselves and others. And if we know what we are headed for it is important to know where we have come from. We can then begin to distinguish personal preferences from biblical commands, seeing what is really important and sharing the privilege of watching others grow in faith and ministry. This *Oasis* focuses on our comings and goings, looking at Ruth, Psalm 139, Matthew and 2 Corinthians. Try to read through the whole of Ruth in one sitting—it's only four chapters and better than Mills and Boon! The *Oasis* is not a psychological study, but as we face up to who we have been, who we are and who we will become we find again that God is there in the honesty, offering refreshment and renewal. And as workers are continually renewed so God will renew and refresh youth and children's work.

✷ Looking back at yourself   Ruth 1

...While they were living there, Elimelech died, and Naomi was left alone with her two sons, who married Moabite women, Orpah and Ruth. About ten years later Mahlon and Chilion also died, and Naomi was left all alone, without husband or sons. (Ruth 1:1–5)

> *To arrive where you are, to get from where you are not,*
> *You must go by a way wherein there is no ecstasy.*

T.S. Eliot, *East Coker*

Whilst separated by some three thousand years, the sheer weight of the situation in which Naomi, Ruth and Orpah found themselves resonates in our contemporary world where, for many, life is still a journey 'wherein there is no ecstasy'. Imagine how Ruth felt looking back over her life: she had joined a family where both her father and new husband had died prematurely. As such these three women were not only alone, but they had no rights to property, no place in society and were far from the only place where they could naturally find support and help, Judah. The book of Ruth does not give us an analysis of Ruth's psychological state, any discussions with her therapist, or recommended course of treatment that she had to help her cope! Long before any such provision, Ruth had to move on and get on with life. Later on in the book we glimpse that part of Naomi's reaction to the loss of sons and husband was to remember and keep her trust in God, setting off home with her daughters-in-law. Perhaps it was this reaction that led Ruth, a Moabite woman, to adopt the faith of Israel, claiming that 'your God will be my God'.

Although the text tells us tantalizingly little of Ruth's own past, what we do have is essential in providing us with the context and background to her present life and faith. As we seek to work with those who are growing in both life and faith, facing and acknowledging our own past provides insight, not only into who we are at present, but also on the action and work of God who created and knows us completely. There may not be answers to all our experiences and questions, those are to be left for another day. But in both mystery and understanding, all can be left with God.

✷ But God   Ruth 1

But Ruth answered, 'Don't ask me to leave you! Let me go with you. Wherever you go, I will go; wherever you live, I will live. Your people will be my people, and your God will be my God. Wherever you die, I will die, and that is where I will be buried. May the Lord's worst punishment come upon me if I let anything but death separate me from you!' (Ruth 1:16–17)

Repentance, the first word in Christian immigration, sets us on the way to travelling in the light. It is a rejection that is also an acceptance, a leaving that develops into an arriving.

Eugene H. Peterson, *The Journey*

'It felt like God just reached into my life,' the 17-year-old explained, 'and pulled out all the crap that was there.'

That is one way of describing an event experienced by millions of people the world over. For Ruth, perhaps in observing Naomi's continued trust in God, her God was now no longer the Moabite Chermosh of human sacrifices, but the faithful, covenant God, Yahweh. Looking back over your own journey of faith it may be that you can identify a time when you became a Christian. Or perhaps it was over a longer period, maybe from birth and upbringing in a loving Christian home. Whichever it was, both the definite event and long-term process are important as God works in many different ways. What is common to both is the response to God's initiative: Ruth saw Naomi's reaction to hearing that 'the Lord had blessed his people with a good harvest'. A danger for many in youth and children's work is that the memory and reality of God's call and initiative is something in the distant past and from which there has been little growth or development. And for some, press-ganged into leadership by busy and desperate churches, there has never been a personal response to God.

But ministry is ineffective and impossible without such a response, and in some ways the whole of the Christian life is exploring, understanding and growing in what happens when we respond to God's initiative. For like Ruth and our teenager, turning to God, away from sin, is a step towards our acceptance and arrival home, in spite of, but more often through, all our life experience.

✳ Knowing me, knowing myself
Psalm 139 and 2 Corinthians 4

Lord, you have examined me and you know me. You know everything I do...
(Psalm 139:1–2)

Men go abroad to wonder at the height of mountains... at the vast compass of the ocean, at the circular motion of the stars; and they pass by themselves without wondering.

St Augustine, *Confessions*

One danger inherent to any exercise in self-examination is lack of balance. When we look at ourselves we may either have too great a consideration of our abilities, power or worth, or, as many teenagers do we focus on negative aspects of our body or character: too fat or thin, big ears, too negative, not generous enough. But how often do we 'wonder at the height of the mountains' but 'pass by' ourselves 'without wondering'? For some of us that ignorance is driven by fear that we don't want anyone else knowing all about us, our inadequacies and weaknesses. However, Psalm 139 points us back to God's all encompassing knowledge of us: our actions, thoughts and words. This knowledge of us, is total; as the psalmist says, 'too deep' and 'beyond my understanding'. However, unlike our fear of letting others know too much about us, God's total knowledge is an assurance of his protection. What sort of person do you think God knows you as? What are you like? Are you like a whirlpool drawing people to yourself, or a garden sprinkler bringing refreshment to others? Perhaps you are more placid, like a still tub of bathwater?

Of course there are many ways of thinking about yourself, and many more attributes of character, all of which can be positive or negative. The whirlpool may also draw others into their negativity and to discouragement, the sprinkler may smother people with too much attention. But greater self-knowledge is helpful if we are in the business of ministering to others. We begin to understand why we are as we are and how we minister most effectively. But, whatever we feel, God's total knowledge of us is truly his power and protection as we are changed, day by day, to be more like Jesus.

✳ A past for the future 2 Corinthians 5:17–18

When anyone is joined to Christ, he is a new being; the old is gone, the new has come. (2 Corinthians 5:17)

...the divine ordinariness of Jesus, and his love for the small and lost and lonely are matters for celebration by everyone.

Adrian Plass, *Learning to Fly*

So often the Christian life is presented as something so new that anything that ever happened before is worthless. In one sense that is true. To be a new creation is to break with our past when 'we were enemies of God' because we are now his friends and engaged in his work. But perhaps there are some areas where such a sense of a great divide is actually inappropriate if we are to catch sight of the full sweep of God's work. The fact that we have changed does not necessarily mean that we have become a completely different person, nor does it signal the fact that everything that we have been up to that point is worthless in God's sight. No, we carry all that we are on into this new existence, our skills, gifts and personality, and find that God actively changes and transforms them. In all Christian people the divine and the ordinary engage, there is no special super-Christian better than the rest. God takes and shapes whatever he finds. I often think how insufferable the church would be if all Christians became perfect overnight!

In writing to the Corinthians, Paul goes on to point out that as God recreates the ordinary in people, the outcome is for ordinary people to be called into the same work of re-creation, 'of making others his friends, too'. Not that we can save anyone, only Jesus is able to do that. Rather, God graciously uses ordinary people in that process. In working with children and young people it is not the Christian super-saints, omniscient of the Bible and youth culture, who are useful to God. It is those who bring their ordinariness, offering it to God to be reshaped with his divinity and for his glory.

✴ Learners who lead or leaders who learn?
Matthew 11

...Take my yoke and put it on you, and learn from me, because I am gentle and humble in spirit; and you will find rest. For the yoke I will give you is easy, and the load I will put on you is light. (Matthew 11:28–30)

Everything I had hoped for came to pass: I returned with more energy than I can remember having since I was fifteen years old... The sabbatical had done its work.

Eugene H. Peterson, *The Gift*

Self-sufficiency, or unwillingness to learn, is like a cancer to both Christian people and Christian ministries. The result is death: the painful tragedy of the public fall or the private descent into stagnant cynicism. Of course, not everyone who is good at anything has such an attitude, but all are prone to it. To become a Christian is to become a learner. It is to take Jesus' yoke upon us. The illustration used by Jesus had instant relevance in an agrarian society where yokes were used by farmers to guide and control the oxen in their daily work. So to learn from Jesus is to be guided and disciplined by him for daily living. But this is no strenuous, overbearing task, but rather one that comes from he who is gentle and humble in heart; it is not so much duty as refreshment. So those involved in ministry, constantly giving to others, must ensure adequate time and space to receive from God. Whether daily, weekly, or, as Peterson describes above, for a longer sabbatical, the flow of life-giving water needs to be constant if we are to avoid stagnation. Jesus pointed his own generation away from the Torah—the law—as the yoke guiding their lives, and pointed towards himself. This was no escape from ethical and spiritual responsibilities—if anything, those are greater (see Matthew 5:20)—but rather a godly rest and learning, because of his nature and character. Rest, refreshment and renewal will only come to those willing to learn from him. When it comes to leadership and learning, it is not a case of either/or but rather both/and.

✴ The future   Ruth 4

So Boaz took Ruth home as his wife. The Lord blessed her, and she became pregnant and had a son. ... Obed became the father of Jesse, who was the father of David. This is the family line from Perez to David: Perez, Hezron, Ram, Amminadab, Nahshon, Salmon, Boaz, Obed, Jesse, David. (Ruth 4:13–22)

The essential thing 'in heaven and earth' is... that there should be long obedience in the same direction.

Friedrich Nietzsche, *Beyond Good and Evil*

As they left the fields of Moab, the future was uncertain. But within a few months, because of the gracious action of their kinsman-redeemer, Boaz, the story has come full circle. Although described in cultural terms so different from our own, a son has been born, weeping has turned to laughter, and uncertainty has been overtaken by a secure and blessed· future. Without knowing their future, the 'long obedience' of Naomi and Ruth resulted in God's blessing and providence being revealed in their lives. Likewise, we too do not know what the immediate future will bring: unemployment, bereavement, a building society windfall. But we do have an assurance, so vividly portrayed in the visionary language of the book of Revelation, that we will 'see the face of God' in a new earth and heaven, where 'we will 'rule as kings for ever' with him. Like two great anchors in the life of the believer, the cross brings certainty of forgiveness and new life, whilst heaven brings certainty of an eternal future with God.

These things do not draw us away from the world into irrelevance, but keep us anchored into whatever life brings, knowing that God has done, and will do, all that is necessary to assure our future with him. Such truths free us for that 'long obedience in the same direction' that, in both life and ministry, should be the joyful response to God's grace and assurance.

For Naomi and Ruth their past and present became an essential part of God's dealings with humankind, as the genealogy shows. To be a forebear of Jesse and David was to be a human forebear of Jesus himself, and through him to all Christian people.

Taking the Plunge

1. In the first chapter of Ruth, what are the different circumstances that make up the context of Naomi's life and faith, and what has she seen and recognized about God in those? (Look at 1:1–5, 6, 8, 17–18, 20–21.) Looking back over your own life, what have been the defining experiences that have affected your life and faith?

2. What changes would happen in Ruth's life as a result of her declaration of allegiance to Naomi and her God? (Look at 1:15–16, 18–19.) When did you first become aware of God's initiative in your own life, and how has it affected you?

3. What weaknesses in Paul did God use to show his 'supreme power'? (Look at 1 Corinthians 2:3–4.) Is there anything about yourself that you are surprised God uses?

4. What is the application of 2 Corinthians 5:17 that Paul reminds his hearers of in verse 16? How might that affect the way in which you see yourself and the children with whom you work?

5. What have you learnt about the following over the past six months: (a) yourself, (b) the Christian life, (c) youth or children's leadership?

6. What do you know about your own life and ministry in the next twelve months? How does God's promise of a secure future, and his proven faithfulness to his people in the past, affect your own immediate future?

Soaking In

Read through Psalm 139, considering each of the statements about God's knowledge and care in relation to yourself. Use this as a basis for a prayer conversation with God about yourself, and who he wants you to become. For instance, 'you know everything I do': talk to God about your own actions, good and bad, giving thanks as appropriate.

As you go through the psalm, continue the conversation. Although there may not be a two-way discussion, some people find it helpful to imagine what God says by speaking the text as the answer to some of their questions. Remember that this should be a positive exercise, not a negative rehearsal of your faults. Thank God for all that you are, and will become, in him.

Overflow

Take time to consider where you have come to in your life and faith so far. Use a spider map to help you remember. You will need an A4 piece of paper. In the centre write your name. Around it write the most significant people and events that have affected your life and faith. Join each one to yourself with a line. As you continue, think about all the links between events and people, and the events and people that are related to those. Do not try to indicate any time-scale, unless you can do good 3D modelling(!), but simply mark all that has brought you to this point now. You may begin to understand a little more about yourself and your ministry, and you will have some fodder for prayer.

Flooded Out!

Any group of people working together in ministry always benefit from a greater knowledge of each other, but it's worth spending time finding the right way to share this information. A humorous way of doing this is to play Consequences together. This well-known game requires everyone to have a piece of paper. The leader asks everyone to write an answer to something. You could start with first names. Everyone now folds the paper over to cover their answers and passes it to the next person. The leader asks another question, answers are written, papers folded and passed on. The process continues until ten questions have been asked. Be careful not to ask questions that are too personal, but rather aim to encourage to get everyone talking. You could include some of the following: what's your favourite food/colour/place? where did you spend your childhood? what would you do if you won the lottery? At the end each paper is unravelled and you can have great fun working out which statement belongs to whom. Remember to end with prayer, giving thanks for everyone.

OASIS 3

Where am I
taking the group?

*Raining again. Ughh! Six months ago, starting some relational youth work from
scratch seemed such a good idea. Meeting kids where they are, listening and
building relationships. The people, the funding, even the enthusiastic backing
from the church council all came together just at the right moment. But that was
then. This is now. And it's still raining. Two hours of hanging about and very little to show for it. There are some really good relationships beginning to develop
between each worker and their own particular group. Even you, with all your
doubts about your ability, have begun to see a group of girls fairly regularly. But
at the back of your mind you can't help wondering where it is all going. No one
really seems to know what you're aiming to do. Will they ever ask questions
about God? What should you say to the young girl in your group who is obviously pregnant?*

*'Wotcha, Gail!' You're wrenched from your thoughts by a thump on your back
as three girls pile over the wall.*

*'You must be mad hanging around here in this weather,' says Tara.
Her bump seems bigger than ever. 'Come on, let's go somewhere.'*

*Allowing yourself to be caught up into the swirling circle
of youthful energy your mind is dragged back into the
immediate. Who knows what the future will bring? That
is then. This is now.*

It has been wisely said that if you aim at nothing, that is
exactly what you will achieve. However, the fashionable
obsession with defined aims, goals and objectives, and all
the associated paraphernalia of mission statements, work
plans, and attainment targets, can be a hindrance as well
as a help to Christian ministry. It is tempting to offer some
'How to…' advice that will lay out clearly the way in which
a successful ministry will go about planning and achieving
its aims and objectives. However, whilst planning, focus and

clarity are vital to good ministry, God's activity is on a much broader and deeper scale than we can imagine. So rather than present a 'How to…' guide of aims and objectives, this *Oasis* will explore these important issues through six aspects of ministry: risk, safety, healing, perfection, toil, obedience. The books of Ezekiel, Colossians and Revelation will be the wells from which we drink and through which we will, once again, find refreshment.

Testing the Water

✳ Risk   Ezekiel 47:1–6

The man led me back to the entrance of the Temple. Water was coming out from under the entrance and flowing east, the direction the Temple faced… With his measuring rod the man measured five hundred metres downstream to the east and told me to wade through the stream there. (Ezekiel 47:1 and 3)

> Heaven shall not wait
> For our legalised obedience,
> Defined by statute, to strict conventions bound:
> Jesus is Lord;
> He has hallmarked true allegiance—
> Goodness appears where his grace is sought and found.
>
> John Bell, *Heaven Shall Not Wait*

Being a prophet involved risk. To speak to the ears of those who directed the affairs of the nation, to the lifestyles and conduct of ordinary people, all involved risk. We tend to think of prophets as those who *fore-told* the future. Whilst this is partly true, the Old Testament prophets also spoke from, and into, the social and political situation of their day, *forth-telling*, relating the truth about God to their society.

Ezekiel straddled the momentous events of 597 and 587BC when Jerusalem was overrun and the nation, probably including Ezekiel himself, was carried into exile. His vision of restoration and redemption also contains risk: risk of non-fulfilment, of disappointment. The idea of the salty, barren area of the Dead Sea becoming fertile was certainly strange to his hearers. But as our 'acted-out parable' in chapter 47 shows, experiencing the promise of abundance and refreshment was only possible for Ezekiel as he was willing to risk being led to the place where the water was so deep that only those willing to swim would survive. If you can experience God's blessing with the water round your ankles, how much more is there for those willing to swim?

C.H. Spurgeon encourages people to 'swim in them; I mean, let us learn to trust God in active exertions for the promotion of his kingdom, to trust him in endeavours to do good!' But how much of our active exertion, our ministry, is 'defined by statute, to strict conventions bound'? 'We've always done it like this.' 'We've tried that before.' 'But think where that might lead us—we don't know what would happen!' Perhaps not in quite those words, but nevertheless, although we face profound changes in church and society, the answer is often the same: play it safe, don't take risks. But Christians stand in a long line of risk-takers whose active exertions have reached new countries and cultures. What they knew, we need to discover: that it is in being willing to take risks that refreshment, goodness and grace are found. These are not the rash, stupid risks that 'play fast and loose' with children's or young people's physical, emotional or spiritual safety. They are the risks of planning and vision that lead to refreshing encounters with God.

Where are you taking your group? You are taking them into risk.

✳ Safety   Ezekiel 47:1–12

He said to me, '...on each bank of the stream all kinds of trees will grow to provide food. Their leaves will never wither, and they will never stop bearing fruit... because they are watered by the stream that flows from the Temple.' (Ezekiel 47:12)

> *Eternal God and Father,*
> *you create us by your power*
> *and redeem us by your love:*
> *guide and strengthen us by your Spirit,*
> *that we may give ourselves in love and service*
> *to one another and to you;*
> *through Jesus Christ our Lord. Amen.*
>
> Collect for use in Morning Prayer, *Alternative Service Book 1980*

As well as being risky, Ezekiel's vision is also profoundly safe. It is not a safety which is born out of comfortable surroundings or reliable security. Rather it is a holy safety. This holy safety is possible because of the source of the river that flows out from the temple. For the Jews, the temple was not simply a place where public worship could be conducted, but a place where the very presence of God dwelt. Thus the implication of Ezekiel's vision is that the source of this water is God himself. Even having shown the massive extent of its refreshing powers, notice the comment towards the end of the passage: 'they will have fresh fruit every month, because they are watered by the stream that flows from the Temple.' Refreshment on this scale was only possible because of its divine source. So in any consideration of aims and objectives, the future direction of the work, it is only possible to step forward in risk if we understand that this is done in the holy safety of God. The prayer reminds us that we can look for the guidance and strength of God, because we acknowledge that the Eternal God creates and redeems us. He is the source of our physical and spiritual life, and thus can bring all that we need for our future life and work. The task of ministry is to mediate the reality of God's safety through the actions and words of leaders and others. And that may mean taking some risks!

Where are you taking your group? You are taking them into safety.

25

✳ Healing   Ezekiel 47:1–12

The trees will provide food, and their leaves will be used for healing people. (Ezekiel 47:12)

Death, decay, entropy, and destruction are the true suspensions of God's laws; miracles are the early glimpses of restoration.

Philip Yancey, *The Jesus I Never Knew*

Much of my childhood and youth was spent in a spa town where, over the years, royalty, socialites and ordinary people had come to the town to 'take the waters'. By the time I was grown up, the baths had gone and there was just one small well left. One more than averagely boring Saturday afternoon, I went with some friends to try the water. It was the most muddy-looking, foul-smelling and evil-tasting concoction I have ever tasted! And it certainly seemed to do me no good at all. In contrast the waters of risk and safety in Ezekiel's vision are, ultimately, the waters of healing. John, perhaps writing some 650 years later, frames another vision in similar terms to that of Ezekiel, perhaps even with Ezekiel's words in his memory as he wrote. In Revelation 21, John's vision of the heavenly city, the river flows within the city nourishing the tree of life that, like Ezekiel's trees, brings life and healing. Both rivers have their source in God, a source that brings about healing and restoration, making possible a return to God. Such healing is assured, completely in John's vision, and partially in Ezekiel's (note, not all of the barren salt water is refreshed). Similar wholeness is made possible through the ministry of Jesus where we can see such 'early glimpses of restoration'. So in looking forward to the future of ministry we are looking toward healing and wholeness, now and in heaven, impacting the way we think, pray, plan and act in our ministry.

Where are you taking your group? You are taking them into healing.

✳ Perfection   Colossians 1:27–28

...And the secret is that Christ is in you, which means that you will share in the glory of God. So we preach Christ to everyone. With all possible wisdom we warn and teach them in order to bring each one into God's presence as a mature individual in union with Christ. (Colossians 1:27–28)

> *It's not that I feel cheated by grace*
> *You freely give: each glimpse of your divine*
> *Perfection crushes me—yet gives a taste*
> *For holiness transcendent, pure, refined.*
> *My worship's still a poor, discordant thing;*
> *But one day I shall see, and I shall sing!*
> D.A. Carson, 'Forty-eight, Destiny', *Holy Sonnets of the Twentieth Century*

To be morally uplifting, to teach the Bible, to make them Christians, to give them somewhere to go, to please their parents, to get them into church, to do better than the church down the road, to satisfy my desire to be needed... the list is endless.

What are you aiming for in your ministry? Do you feel you are meeting any of your aims?

Writing to the Christians at Colossae in the Lycus Valley, Paul sets out the exact nature of his mission. It seems that some form of bad teaching had taken hold. A different modern translation suggests it may have been, 'You need Jesus *plus* some new special wisdom, which we will tell you.' But for Paul, what we preach is Christ— nothing more, nothing less. In setting out his mission, and that of all Christian ministers, Paul makes a startling claim about his aims and objectives. He does not aim simply to strengthen the church (although that may happen), to spread his own reputation, or to please his hearers. He aims to bring them 'mature' or 'perfect in Christ' before God. What's more, it seems that this is following the pattern of God's mission to the world seen in Jesus.

Looking back to verse 22, God seeks to 'make you his friends, in order to bring you holy, pure and faultless, into his presence'. In the original, the words 'to bring' (v. 22) and 'to bring each one' (v. 28) are different forms of the same verb. Wow! Whatever you do with children and young people you are called to follow God's example in Jesus. It should ultimately aim to bring them mature and perfect before Jesus himself at the last day. The 'crushing perfection' of God will someday be mirrored in those who seek to serve and follow him, including the children and young people with whom you work. Its downpayment is with us now: 'Christ is in you.' Then we shall all 'see' and 'sing'.

Where are you taking your group? You are taking them into perfection.

✳ Toil   Colossians 1:28—29

So we preach Christ to everyone. With all possible wisdom we warn and teach them in order to bring each one into God's presence as a mature individual in union with Christ. (Colossians 1:28)

Your task is to keep telling the basic story, representing the presence of the Spirit, insisting on the priority of God, speaking the biblical words of command and promise and invitation.

Eugene H. Peterson, *The Gift*

To move towards maturity in Christ, Paul speaks of doing three basic activities: proclaiming, warning, teaching. Just as a triangle needs three corners to exist, so all three go together to make the whole. In the face of many competing models, it is vital that youth and children's ministry does not lose the focus in these three activities. But they are not easy; they are not quick-fix solutions. For Paul it was 'toil' and 'struggle' to proclaim, warn and teach. But it is the way to maturity. The exact shape of proclamation, warning and teaching is not prescribed here. True, it is all about Christ, and follows the example of God, but it will take as many forms as there are different types of ministry. Nevertheless, at some point we must 'retell the basic story', to 'preach Christ'. It may be in a different form from previous generations, but it must be done. We must avoid the temptation to shy away from saying the hard truths to people in order to gain their adulation, or the temptation to teach what will be acceptable and pleasing to the desires rather than the needs. Such ministry may be amongst many—'we warn and teach *them*'—but must be rooted in individual relationship and encounter— 'bring *each one*'. Such is God's care for the individual. And so toil and striving cease to become a sign that it is going wrong, or that we are failing. It could just be that it is the sign of God at work, that truth is being shared, and that the first few, faltering steps towards perfection are being taken.

Where are you taking your group? You are taking them through toil.

✷ Obedience   Colossians 1:29

To get this done I toil and struggle, using the mighty strength which Christ supplies and which is at work in me. (Colossians 1:29)

I am speaking of a leadership in which power is constantly abandoned in favour of love...

Henri Nouwen, *In the Name of Jesus*

Ezekiel's great vision, John's panoramic apocalypse, Paul's great mission to the known world. It makes you exhausted just thinking about it! It seems to be the stuff of spiritual giants, great leaders in the faith, of whom we can only ever be a poor reflection. But to believe that would be to rob them, and the gospel, of its secret and strength. Because each one knew that it was not in their own strength, but 'using the mighty strength which Christ supplies' that such obedience and faithfulness were possible. The obedience that is exercised in Christian leadership is not one of slavishly following a prescribed system, a series of exercises towards spiritual power. Rather it is one where power is constantly abandoned in favour of love. Obedience expressed in this way discovers that Christ supplies his mighty strength to continue laying aside everything. As youth and children's ministry has developed over the years, much of the work, although driven by good motives, has actually been an exercise of power and control over those we seek to lead. We want them to perform, to act in ways that we think will please God, whilst knowing in our secret selves that such response is mainly geared to pleasing our own feelings of self worth. The tragedy is that such a leadership neither acknowledges that Christ is in those we seek to lead, nor follows the example of him who came as a servant and was obedient to death. It will also stifle the moments where growth and maturity take hold, as the led learn to listen to God and become the leaders. We need a style of leadership that is radically focused on Jesus, where obedience is expressed in the abandoning of power and where the creative love of God is discovered in all and through all.

Where are you taking your group? You are taking them to the place where you can both be led into obedience.

Taking the Plunge

1. Imagine that you are Ezekiel being led out into the stream. What words and thoughts come to mind as you are led forward? To what extent is your own life and ministry characterized by godly risk-taking?
2. What does this vision tell us of God's character? In what ways are you aware of personally, and seek to offer, the safety of God?
3. How have you experienced God's healing? To what extent, and how, do you encourage and expect God to heal yourself and those you serve?
4. Do you think Paul was unrealistic in his aims? What is your own experience of setting aims and objectives in your ministry? Did you achieve them?
5. When did you last (a) proclaim the truth, (b) teach the truth, or (c) warn someone

in the light of the truth? Is there a difference between 'warning' and being judgmental?

6. How could you learn to be more obedient in laying aside power? Why do we find it so hard to allow children and young people to take the lead?

Soaking In

Imagine that you had to write your own obituary for publication. You have been asked to give particular focus to your work with children or young people, on what you achieved etc. If writing doesn't suit you, just use notes, or imagine it in your head. But, if you can, try to write it down, refine it and work on it. Use it as a tool to assess where you have got to with your work amongst children and young people. When you have finished, try to find someone who knows you and your work, ask them to read it with you and talk about the issues it raises.

Overflow

When thinking about aims and objectives it can be easy to lose sight of individuals. Why not have a board up at home with photographs of group members and leaders on it? If you have it somewhere where you see it regularly it will remind you to pray for them. You may want to copy out Colossians 1:28–29 and put it there to remind you of the task. Make sure that you set aside some time each week to pray for them and to ask that God would bring restoration, renewal and refreshment to their lives.

Flooded Out!

As a team, make sure you set aside time to think about your aims and objectives, building in times for review. There are many tools available to help you with this; perhaps someone in your church can help.

One interesting way to monitor planning is to make up a shoebox containing pictures and other memorabilia that describe your work as it now is. Also put into the box a statement about where you see the work going in the future. Give the 'time-capsule' to someone who you know will be around in, say, three years, with strict instructions to give it to the group leaders at that time. It will be fascinating and informative for whoever opens the box, and may teach you something about the development of your ministry.

ASIS 4

Strength and weakness

It had been building up for a few weeks. One group of lads playing table-football, and the new group, skulking by the door. The eyes that made contact across the crowded room were not those of love, but daggered looks of suspicion and hate. Thus far, you and the other leaders have been able to contain the situation; things have not got out of hand. But all attempts at reconciliation seem to fail, neither group willing to articulate their feelings, other than that they alone have the right to be there. It is their club. This evening was different, almost as if they had come determined that it should be sorted once and for all. As you are chatting with some of the younger kids hanging around outside, a leader sticks their head round the door and calls your name.

'Jim,' says Aisha, 'I think you'd better come in here...'

As you re-enter the hall you are confronted by the sight of two lads, each from a different group, eyeballing each other, head to head. You step between them, not knowing what to do or say. All the advice you received on the county training course about physical contact, conflict resolution, and first aid, swims randomly round your mind. How do you show God's love and not get walked over? What does it mean to serve these lads? As you open your mouth to speak, a fist hurtles past your left ear and makes contact with flesh somewhere behind you...

Ask any group of people what makes a good leader and you will get a multitude of different answers. Some will suggest great strength of character, others focus on personal skills to inspire and motivate. In many ways their answer will depend on the job within which leadership is to be exercised. In the scenario above, you might need a different set of skills than those required of someone working with senior citizens, that is unless the bingo gets ugly! This *Oasis* will consider what it means to be a strong Christian leader and how that might impact upon the ministries we exercise. First, we'll look at strength shown in our reaction to external impacts. Second, strength will be seen in what comes from within the leader to those being led. Our way into the whole of this subject will be through the picture of the suffering servant of Isaiah, Paul's second letter to the Corinthians, and his advice to Timothy.

30

✳ Brokenness, the well of strength   Isaiah 53:5

We are healed by the punishment he suffered, made whole by the blows he received. (Isaiah 53:5)

> *Our only health is the disease*
> *If we obey the dying nurse*
> *Whose constant care is not to please*
> *But to remind of our, and Adam's curse,*
> *And that, to be restored, our sickness must*
>   *grow worse.*
>
> T.S. Eliot, *East Coker*

We cannot be entirely certain whom the writer of Isaiah 53 had in mind as he sketched this somewhat enigmatic portrait of the suffering servant. A traditional interpretation has been to see the person and work of Jesus prefigured here. As such there is a great depth of Christian theology to be found in this passage concerning the nature of salvation. But the New Testament also commends Jesus as an example to be followed, and that is the angle which we shall explore. The word translated 'punishment' holds a double meaning, conveying ideas of both peace and punishment. Thus healing comes through suffering, the blows upon the servant bringing wholeness. In obeying 'the dying nurse', following in Jesus' footsteps, we too need to be broken: all within us that promotes and relies on self as the way to greatness must be dismantled, not in self-flagellating pity, but in order that we may be rebuilt upon Jesus. Of course, we will not be broken in order to bring salvation to the whole world; only Jesus could achieve that. Nevertheless it is through brokenness that we become available to God and are in a position to be able to receive his correcting care. To look at some youth and children's ministry you might be fooled into thinking it was a matter of strength, beauty, ability, youth or even trendiness. However, the truth is that only through those who are willing to be broken can God bring healing and wholeness to both minister and ministry. After all, it is only those who have truly been thirsty who grasp the real value and effect of fresh, pure water. To discover brokenness is truly to discover the well of strength for ministry.

✳ Inside to out, the true defence

Isaiah 53:1–3

He had no dignity or beauty to make us take notice of him. (Isaiah 53:2)

The power of godliness lies in the actions of the soul; take care that you do not stick to the vain, deluding form.

Richard Baxter, *The Saints' Everlasting Rest*

To see the servant was not to see beauty. To see the servant was not to comprehend dignity. To judge by the outward appearance is always wrong, for God looks on the heart. To believe that effective youth and children's ministers must conform to some outward image is a failure to follow Jesus. As he lay dying, Richard Baxter wrote *The Saints' Everlasting Rest* to his large congregation at Kidderminster. His ministry is a high point of both Anglican and non-conformist history (following his reluctant departure from the Church of England). Throughout the turbulent years of the seventeenth century, during civil war, regicide, and the difficulties of the establishing national church, he understood that the secret to true godliness and ministry lies in the 'actions of the soul', not in any 'vain deluding form'. His personal commitment to this, spending time fostering his relationship with God, led to the conversion of over 5,000 people in the small market town of Kidderminster, a national influence in church and state, and a level of ecumenical generosity that was years ahead of his time. He was a true spiritual giant, although to see him would no doubt have been to see simply a man amongst men. To follow the call of Jesus is to be called to the actions of the soul. This is not a withdrawal from activity, but a call to God-driven activity. The secret lies not in what is seen from the outside, but, as with the servant, in the extent to which we attend to the inside.

✳ Acceptance or abuse,
the unreasonable reaction   Isaiah 53:7

He was treated harshly, but endured it humbly; he never said a word.
(Isaiah 53:7)

The very things that plunder hope, these are what God uses to accomplish his purposes.
Philip Yancey, *The Jesus I Never Knew*

'Harsh treatment' are words that are part of the experience of almost every youth or children's worker: unthankful children and teenagers, parents looking for someone to blame, the church that wants to see 'bums on seats'. How should we react when the actions of others seem like abuse? Our own fragile egos cry out against the perceived injustice, seeking to respond in a way that enables us to cling on to some dignity or self-esteem. We think that in that way we are building up our own strength and ability. Yet here we find harsh treatment, but also humble endurance. Alec Motyer has described these verses as the 'climax of Old Testament and biblical soteriology'. That is, that they are at the heart of what the Bible tells us of God's rescue plan for his world. Indeed, for those familiar with the gospels, we hear echoes of Jesus' trial and crucifixion. Harsh treatment; humble endurance. Through humble endurance, the humanly-speaking unreasonable reaction to harsh treatment, God brings forgiveness and healing through the servant. There was no other way for Jesus than the way to the cross. This is not to advocate a style of ministry that 'puts up' and 'shuts up' at every point. But it is to remind us that every time we are tempted to resort to the excuse to escape, the sarcastic rejoinder, or some other form of self-protection we should have the image of the servant and Jesus before us. It is in the things that seem to 'plunder hope', the harsh treatment, the punishment, and the blows, that the purpose of God will succeed.

✳ Death comes to stay, the unyielding life
2 Corinthians 4:8–12

At all times we carry in our mortal bodies the death of Jesus, so that his life also may be seen in our bodies. (2 Corinthians 4:10)

The cross of horror became the cross of hope, the tortured body became the body that gives new life; the gaping wounds became the source of forgiveness, healing and reconciliation.

Henri Nouwen, *Show Me the Way*

To follow Jesus in humble endurance may be seen as simply following the example of a moral teacher (although the context in Isaiah reveals differences). But Paul shows that it is so much more. At a risk of getting technical, there are some things which are important to notice in 2 Corinthians 4:10 and 11. First, Paul uses an unusual word. When he speaks of death Paul normally uses the word *'thanatos'* (as he does in verse 11), but in verse 10 he uses a different word: *'nekrosis'*. This word focuses on the 'way of making dead' or, as C.K. Barrett translates, 'we are always carrying about in the body the killing of Jesus'. So Paul suggests that his sufferings are the same sufferings that marked the cross of Jesus. But, lest this should seem morbid or depressing, an important little word, *'hena'*—'in

order that'—shows us why this is such a source of encouragement and strength. The sufferings in ministry, which were very real for Paul and for many of us, are *'in order that* his life may be seen' in our mortal bodies. They are not simply noble acts of moral imitation. As Christian ministers suffer, the life of Jesus is being shown in them. Life is brought out of death. We are seeing the start of God's new age, his kingdom. So in defence of his own suffering and weaknesses in the face of criticism from the self-exalting Corinthian Christians, Paul shows that, as death comes to stay in our ministries, so the unyielding life of God is made known in us. For 'God, who raised the Lord Jesus to life, will also raise us up with Jesus and take us together with you, into his presence.'

✳ Kindness, goodness, patience,
the irresistible current   2 Timothy 2:23–26

As the Lord's servant, you must not quarrel. You must be kind towards all, a good and patient teacher. (2 Timothy 2:24)

Be the living expression of God's kindness—kindness in your face, kindness in your eyes, kindness in your smile, kindness in your warm greeting. In the slums we are the light of God's kindness to the poor.

Mother Teresa of Calcutta, *In the Silence of the Heart*

Kindness, goodness and patience were probably in short supply amongst the Christian community in Ephesus. From what we can know from 1 and 2 Timothy false teachers had a disruptive effect on

their faith and life. Paul had a uneasy visit, leaving quickly, but instructed Timothy to remain and build up the local church. It is into this context of quarrelling and disagreement that he writes in 2 Timothy, urging kindness, goodness and patience, especially to those with whom he differed. Anyone who works with children and young people knows of the potential for disagreement and 'foolish and ignorant arguments'. They can come from anywhere: misguided doctrine, other religions, pet theories, or ignorance. They are held on to tenaciously as those younger in years seek to thrash out their own beliefs and independence from other inherited ideologies and systems. Kindness, goodness and patience can be in short supply. Paul's goal is clear, the original text framing it as a question: 'Will God give them an opportunity for a change of heart?' That is our hope, and so in God's hands gentleness, kindness and patience become his tools to work in the lives of others. In becoming the 'living expression of God's kindness', you reveal God to those whom you serve. Note that the Bible does not advocate quelling inquisitiveness, nor does it discourage questioning. We must encourage such things if young people are to grow into maturity. If openness, gentleness, kindness and patience are hallmarks of our Christian service, then the whole activity is infused with the possibility of God working through us, bringing people to repentance and a knowledge of the truth.

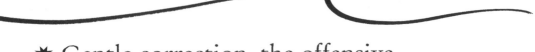

✳ Gentle correction, the offensive weapon   2 Timothy 2:23–26

A ...patient teacher, gentle as you correct your opponents. (2 Timothy 2:24–25)

No cask holds two kinds of drink at the same time. If the cask is to hold wine, its water must first be poured out, leaving the cask empty and clean. If you are to have divine joy, all your creatures must first be poured or thrown out.

Meister Eckhart, *Meister Eckhart*

Looking up the word 'correction' in a thesaurus does not immediately bring gentleness to mind. 'Admonish', 'blue-pencil'(!), 'debug', 'improve', 'punish', 'regulate' or 'reprove' all have austere connotations reminiscent of stern schoolteachers. 'But surely,' we say, 'a good teacher or leader must have strong discipline and firmness?' Well, Paul is not saying that such things are not part of ministry, but remember that his focus is always Jesus. To minister is to follow in Jesus' footsteps, being conformed to his character, and to enable that formation in the lives of those we serve. In the hands of God, gentle correction becomes an offensive weapon. This is one reason why it can be especially hard for some professional educators moving into voluntary or full-time Christian ministry. Similar activities are pursued, but with a completely different set of ground rules. There is a question here as to who the 'opponents' are: they may be those from whom the false teaching has its origin, or simply those caught up in it. This is a difficult issue, but it is likely that in some way both are included. As those caught up are corrected, so the leaders may be changed as well. Whichever it is, the emphasis is that gentle correction is only useful in God's hands, and in his strength. It is not simply a good, moral or nice attitude, but an offensive weapon that is used—wherever the example and instruction of ordinary Christians are shared—to reveal the divine truth of God.

Taking the Plunge

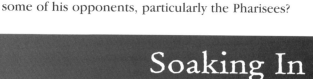

1. Read Isaiah 53:4–6. What could God achieve through the brokenness of the servant? What might this passage tell us about: (a) Jesus, (b) ourselves, (c) our ministry?

2. How might verses 1–3 be mirrored in the life of Jesus? To what extent is personal charisma important in your ministry?

3. What 'harsh treatment' do we find in the life of the servant (53:1–12) and that of Jesus? Why do the servant, and Jesus, choose the path of humble endurance?

4. Have you ever felt as if you were suffering because of your ministry or work with children and young people? If so, what was it like? How does Paul's belief about his own suffering in 2 Corinthians 4:10 affect his interpretation of what has happened to him in verses 8–9? How does this apply to your ministry?

5. How are the values of kindness, goodness and patient teaching reflected in your work with children or young people?

6. When did you last try to 'gently correct' one of the children or young people with whom you work? Is there a tension between this attitude and the way Jesus dealt with some of his opponents, particularly the Pharisees?

Soaking In

For this exercise you will need to find a stone or rock. Aim to find one that fits well into your hand, making sure it is an interesting shape (i.e. not too smooth). This will be used as a way of helping us *focus* our prayer. Note that this is very different from an object that is prayed *to*.

In quietness, roll the stone over in your hand, feeling all the bumps, angles and smooth surfaces. Feel where pieces have been knocked off, broken, or smoothed out. As you continue, begin to think about yourself. What is there that God needs to smooth out in you? In what ways have you been broken by God? How has that affected who you are, and what you offer in ministry? As you continue to hold the stone consider how the following words relate to you: brokenness, humility, death, life, goodness, kindness, patience, inner godliness, gentle correction. As you do so, read again the passages related to each one and ask God to change you to become more like him.

Keep hold of the stone, put it on your mantelpiece, or by your bed, in fact anywhere where it will remind you that you are being constantly reshaped by God for his purposes. If you know other leaders, you may like to swap stones and use theirs as a reminder to pray for that person!

Overflow

Issues relating to strengths and weaknesses often benefit from help from someone outside our situation, who
has some knowledge about us and whom we see more
than once. So why not consider having someone to whom
you can talk regularly about your ministry and life? Ideally
this would be someone in your own congregation, but might also be from elsewhere.
For many years Christians from many different traditions have had spiritual directors,
soul friends, counsellors, pastors, friends... call them what you will! Perhaps a good
place to start would be to talk to your church minister, who might be able to suggest
someone to approach, or who may do it for you.

Flooded Out!

Some training activities for leaders are too 'precious' and meaningful—so here's one to
put a stop to that! But, before you look elsewhere, remember that most people learn
best through activity and experience, so why not try it? Don't be put off by an active activity—it's not just for fit types. The greater the variety of people, the more you will learn.
In the week before the meeting ask your leaders to use as many of the 'Testing the Water'
sections from this *Oasis* as possible. Make sure that you warn your leaders to come wearing trousers and old clothes: cassocks or skirts are not recommended! You need to
arrange for a piece of rope (preferably 'bungee' or elasticated) to be tied, or held,
between two points at about waist height. The aim is to get the whole group from one
side of the rope to the other, without going around or under it (i.e. they must all go
over). The group must travel *en masse*, i.e. there must be constant physical connection
between all participants. If this connection breaks down, or anyone touches the cord or
breaks the 'force field' under the cord, the whole group must restart.

At the end of the activity the following questions may be helpful:
* *What were the strengths and weaknesses of the group members? How was each of
them seen and used? Were any complementary?*
* *Did anyone feel embarrassed? (Discuss in pairs.)*
* *Thinking about the experience, what do the following words have
to say to us as a team of leaders? (In pairs, think of one comment and one thing to learn.)*

> *Brokenness, humility, death, life, goodness, patience,
> kindness, inner godliness, gentle correction.*
> *(Remember to encourage people to look for the posi-
> tive things. Depending on the time available, you may
> want to give each pair two words.)*
> *Is there anything in this exercise specific to the age
> group whom you serve?*

This would be a great exercise to do twice, with a six-
month gap in between. Remember it's progress, not perfection, that matters!

OASIS 5

Plugging In ...

Relationships

By now you are strangely used to the silence. It no longer surprises you that the youth group have nothing to say. In the rare moments when they do say something their vocabulary seems strictly limited to either 'yes' or 'no'. There's animated discussion over coffee, biscuits being thrown around, people being hugged, thumped or attacked. But as soon as you try to get the session started, inactivity descends, and silence takes over. The lively teaching material that got you excited during the week rapidly takes on the consistency of super-cooled school custard. Even a session on sex, normally guaranteed for at least a titter, gets completely bogged down. But then, at the end of the session things are like they were at the beginning—smiles, laughter and chat. After the session you and the other leader, Sam, sit down and review. As you talk, Sam asks if you know what is wrong with one of the lads who seems particularly depressed. It slowly dawns on you both that you have not got a clue and, even worse, you wouldn't even know where to start. In fact you can't remember the last time you actually talked to him. Might this have something to do with the way the whole group has been recently?

Youth and children's work is relational. If it is not rooted in real relationships, it is not Christian ministry with children and young people. This is so because, as Andrew Walker has observed, 'the Christian story is insistent that God is personal by nature', rooted in 'the Trinitarian relatedness' of God. God is in relationship and, in his image, our relationships are to be a refreshing, sharing celebration of all that God is. Too much ministry goes astray either because of the lack of relationships or because of relationships in which God's image is marred. For leaders, as we enter and reflect on the relatedness of God, there are certain skills and responsibilities that are important in the relationships that form the core of our ministry. In this *Oasis* we will look at six key aspects of relationships in the craft of ministry that, if handled wisely, will lead to better youth and children's ministry: love, attention, impartiality, space, sexuality and power. But each of these swords is definitely two-edged and, as our explorations of Luke, John, and 1 Corinthians will reveal, if handled incorrectly can be disastrous in their effect.

✳ Love John 4:1–42

It was about noon. A Samaritan woman came to draw some water, and Jesus said to her, 'Give me a drink of water.' (John 4:6–7)

This is the age in which the walls come down. Each one of us is going to have to go beyond what makes us comfortable if we are going to put the human back into humanity.

Mike Riddell, *alt.spirit@metro.m3*

It is easy to talk about love. The language of love is one around which Christians of all backgrounds can unite. But what do we mean by it? What is our experience of it? How is it reflected in ministry and mission? In his encounter with the Samaritan woman Jesus redefines love. Although Jews and Samaritans were geographically neighbours, in every other way they were miles apart. As R.E.O. White has pointed out, this woman 'formed, in the first century, an unorthodox, rival fringe of Judaism, alienated, suspected, and despised.' But John goes further—note the time: 'It was about noon.' In a hot, eastern climate, noon was not the time to go and draw water. That is, unless you were not an accepted member of the community. A Samaritan and an adulteress. Most Jewish men would pray daily,

'Blessed art thou O Lord… who hast not made me a woman'. To publicly acknowledge, converse with and accept water from this woman was significant. Jesus' ministry amongst those on the outside, on the wrong side of prejudice, provides a pattern to be followed by all. Often youth or children's ministry justifies the subtle rejection of the outsider. 'Those lads are just more trouble than we can cope with.' 'This child disrupts the session for others.' All the while we are often saying, 'You don't conform to the sort of people we like to work with, so go away, please.' Love can only be offered if, as John says, we know we have been loved by God. The love we can then offer is a strong, fierce, joyful, committed love, that dares to take the walls down and go beyond comfort through, and in, the name of Jesus.

✳ Attention John 4:1–42

Jesus answered, 'If only you knew…' Jesus answered, 'Whoever drinks this water…' Jesus replied, 'You are right when you say…' Jesus said to her, 'Believe me, woman…' Jesus answered, 'I am he, I who am talking with you.' (John 4:10–26)

He who can no longer listen to his brother will soon be no longer listening to God either; he will be doing nothing but prattle in the presence of God too

Dietrich Bonhoeffer, *Life Together*

As I write these words, many mourn the tragic loss of Diana, Princess of Wales. The quasi-religious language in which she has been described—'a saviour', 'a light in the world', 'a saint'—has often focused on her

ability to give attention. Listening to those who received from her, it seems it was not her fame, power or glory that struck them, but simply that she, an imperfect human being, gave genuine attention.

Imagine a film crew recording the exchange between Jesus and the Samaritan woman: the close up face shots, the woman looking away, the gaze of Jesus, a shot of nervous hands, the intimate setting, the drink offered. The whole scene speaks of attention. Not simply of one human to another, but more, the intimate attention of God. And all focused on this flawed outcast. But then God always liked such people. Note the way the conversation is conducted: intimacy, statement, question, answer, statement, command, reply. There is a genuine exchange and mutuality and, although Jesus has insight that is not normally given to us, he is able to weave God's story into the woman's story. Thus attention does not become simply listening, or sycophancy, but a dynamic activity where the Christian story interacts with what is shared and offered. Physical objects—a well, a woman, a mountain—provide natural touching points with God's larger story: Jesus' offer of life-giving water, the insight about marriage, and the natural discussion about worship—the big issue between Jews and Samaritans at that time centred around where true worship should take place: in the temple in Jerusalem (Jews) or on Gerizim (Samaritans).

In our accelerated age, where speed and shallowness have become synonymous, we need to recover the pastoral art of giving attention. With children and young people we must listen and learn the mutual art of story-making. It takes time and effort. But it also provides an environment within which the human and divine stories mingle and where all, like the woman, can know that 'I am he, I who am talking with you'.

✴ Space   Luke 6:27–31

Love your enemies, do good to those who hate you, bless those who curse you, and pray for those who ill-treat you. If anyone hits you on one cheek, let him hit the other one too; if someone takes your coat, let him have your shirt as well. (Luke 6:27–29)

Forgiving love is a possibility only for those who know that they are not good, who feel themselves in need of divine mercy.

Reinhold Niebuhr, *An Interpretation of Christian Ethics*

Using the word 'space' here is not to refer to the physical environment within which you work, but the spiritual, emotional, intellectual and moral space that is created within any youth or children's ministry. Christian ministry has often tried to restrict such space given to people, and thus only reaches those within culturally acceptable standards. It is almost as if the church might become polluted by contact with normal people. The whole function of the church is to recognize that in the mercy and grace of God the limits of the space within which faith can be found and shared are boundless. That is not to say that God condones those who disobey him: the 'enemy' and the 'persecutor'. But the radical command of Jesus is to say, 'There is space here for both of us.' That space should be clear in our deeds ('love', 'do good'), words ('bless') and prayers ('pray for'). The mistake of the rabbis was to cheapen the law's demand for love. For example, 'Love your neighbours, hate your enemies' as in Matthew 5:43 misses out 'love your neighbours *as yourselves*' and narrows its extent by adding 'hate your enemies'.

39

How much work with children or young people also cheapens and restricts the loving, holy space that Jesus calls for? Almost more than at any other age, children and young people need space to challenge, fail, grow, question, triumph, be, cry, laugh and talk. At times, creating space for them will conflict with our own beliefs and expectations. However, practising the pastoral art of space-creation is to create a space where the love and forgiveness of God can be found.

✳ Impartiality   Matthew 5:43–48

If you speak only to your friends, have you done anything out of the ordinary? (Matthew 5:47)

The need to ensure the safety of young people can dictate an atmosphere which prevents those whose lifestyle does not yet fit from joining the church, despite the fact that God is at work in their lives.

Pete Ward, *Growing Up Evangelical*

The model of pastoral care that Jesus sets before us in Matthew 5 and Luke 6 is that of discipleship. It represents a radical alternative to the way in which the world operates and one in which the rewards, results and refreshment are incredible: '…so that you may become the sons of your father in heaven'. Our love, attention and space are to be characterized by an impartiality that sees beyond the immediate lifestyle or circumstances of the individual concerned. In doing so we are entering into the mission and ministry of God, 'just as your Father in heaven is perfect'. It is not a call to the impossible, but a call to a different, subversive, way of living. Where love subverts hate, the ignored and betrayed find holy attention, and those outside conventional restrictions find the space to exist, all marked by an impartiality that joyfully draws all people into the kingdom. Such a commitment to impartiality is a commitment to courage and hard work. It is not an easy stand to take and it is one that inevitably brings misunderstanding and criticism from within, and without, the Christian community. To balance the understandable desire of the church to protect children and young people of faith with the call to be impartial toward those who threaten such protection requires godly wisdom. This is not a simple issue, but all too often we either fail to answer the question, or implicitly state that God cannot overcome the problems, evidenced in our failure to act. But to apply impartiality in youth or children's ministry is to work in the image of God, and make progress toward perfection.

✳ Sexuality   1 Corinthians 10:1–13

Those who think they are standing firm had better be careful that they do not fall. (1 Corinthians 10:12)

There is no such thing as 'safe' sex: the whole thing is highly dangerous. If there is trust and compassion; if there is gentleness and consideration; if there is passion and adventure; if there is intimacy and responsibility: then sex is a sign of God.

Mike Riddell, *alt.spirit@metro.m3*

Have you ever thought that your sexuality is one of the tools that is used, both consciously and unconsciously, in ministry? Children and young people will note the extent to which you are at ease with your own body, the way in which you conduct your personal relationships, the signs of 'special' friends in your life, and they may question your own sexual practices and your views on marriage, divorce and singleness. Given the destructive effects of adultery, or the unrealistic and harmful relationships between unwise leaders and teenagers with crushes, how leaders handle their sexuality is a key issue. The Corinthian church had allowed their super-spirituality to lull them into a false sense of security. 'It will never happen here' driven by spiritual superiority led to covetousness, immorality and idolatry, to name but a few. They had much good to offer, but their presumptuousness had allowed sin, including sexual sin, to gain a foothold. So Paul's warning, rooted in examples from the Old Testament, comes not as an empty phrase exhorting moral behaviour, but a call to those for whom sin had ceased to matter, to wake up and see the reality of their actions. There is no such thing as 'safe sex'; it is an inherently dangerous, but beautifully joyful, business.

This is not to make the mistake of thinking that Christians dislike bodies and sex. We love them both! Paul has already shown in chapter 6:12–20 that bodies are not simply in God's image, but are the very place where 'he lives', so we are to use them 'for his glory' (6:20). Each act of our ministry, the offer of a lift home, personal time spent one-to-one, the touch that lingers, offering care, offers a space where our sexuality becomes a vehicle for truth and learning. As well as intimacy and embrace there will be times when the creative, helpful path will be one of withdrawal, restraint and redirection. For the wise will watch themselves carefully, realizing that the godly sometimes restrict their own freedom so that others might be set free.

✳ Power   1 Corinthians 9:1–15

But I haven't made use of any of these rights, nor am I writing this now in order to claim such rights for myself. I would rather die first! (1 Corinthians 9:15)

Ministerial leadership is first, and finally, discipleship.

Lesslie Newbigin, *The Gospel in a Pluralist Society*

We live in an age when much has been made of rights. Many of these rights are indeed helpful and have been instruments of protection for those on the fringes of society. Talk of rights was not far from the Corinthian church to which Paul had occasion to write several times. One of the themes central to the letter of 1 Corinthians is that of freedom: what does it mean for the Christian, and how did it relate to Paul's rights? The Corinthians certainly seemed to feel that Paul was not exercising his apostleship in the way they believed he should. They saw, in the words of David Prior, 'Christian leadership in terms of being masters, not servants'. And so Paul lays out his rights, but says that he has put them aside 'in order not to put any obstacle in the way of the Good News about Christ'. Power was voluntarily laid aside so that God's strength and his gospel might be made known. Ministry, especially amongst children and young people, provides opportunities to exercise power. At each step the way to mature leadership will involve learning how to lay aside power in order to both protect those we serve and to ensure that all may 'share in the blessings' of the gospel.

In the early days of Billy Graham's evangelistic team a mutual agreement was made to 'downplay the offering and depend as much as possible on money raised by local committees', not to 'travel, meet or eat alone with a woman other than my wife', 'to cooperate with all who would cooperate with us in the public proclamation of the gospel' and 'to top integrity in our publicity and our reporting'. That commitment to mutual accountability and integrity in the exercise of power and rights has lasted through fifty years of international ministry notably free from scandal. For whether it is Paul, Billy Graham, or you and me, the public exercise of power within our ministry is no more than the outworking of our private life with God. It soon becomes clear that first, and finally, leadership is discipleship.

Taking the Plunge

1.   Is there any leader or child you know who would fit into the same category as the Samaritans? What might they find hardest to love in you? How might John 4 affect your approach to that person?
2.   In what ways is the attention that Jesus gives: (a) compassionate, (b) confrontational, (c) challenging? What parts of the Christian story do you find hardest to relate to the lives and situation of the children or young people with whom you work?
3.   Read Matthew 5:43. Does your ministry cheapen or restrict the demands of Jesus? To what extent does creating space for young people inevitably lead to compromising Christian standards?
4.   Is there a tension between impartiality and the need to disciple and mentor individual children and young people?
5.   What does Paul imply should have been expected of God's people in the Old Testament in 1 Corinthians 10:1–4? Using them as an example, why does Paul encourage the Corinthians towards purity? (See vv. 11–12.) What are (a) the opportunities and (b) the dangers for your own sexuality in relationship to the children and young people with whom you work? Can God's promise in verse 13 help us?
6.   Read 1 Corinthians 9:1–15. Why does Paul lay aside his rights to power? (See also verses 19–23). What power and rights do you think you exercise in your ministry?

Soaking In

Look again at John 4. Make yourself comfortable and imagine the scene. Situated halfway between Jerusalem and the hill-country of Galilee, Sychar is set in the hills between the River Jordan and the sea. The low hills are brown and parched. Imagine the searing heat in the middle of the day, the dusty road into the town, and the well. You are standing some way off and see a man with his back to you sitting on the large, flat stones surrounding the well. Imagine the woman coming to draw water, dressed in country clothes, her head covered with a long scarf, a large water pot ready to draw.

Imagine the conversation, spoken in everyday language of ordinary people: intimacy, statement, question, answer, statement, command, reply. Read the text again slowly as the images form in your mind. After a while ask yourself some questions. How is love shown? What sort of attention is shared? Where is space given? Who is impartial? What is the interplay of sexuality and power? Draw insights from a prayerful, imaginative exploration of the text, not from your own invention. You will then have material that you may need to apply to yourself and pray through.

The extract from a prayer below may be a helpful way to end this exercise. It was written in the fourteenth century by Ludolf of Saxony.

Direct my thoughts and words and actions
according to your commandments, O God most high,
that, doing your will in all things,
I may be preserved both here and in eternity.

Overflow

A good way to develop greater self-understanding of your pastoral care is to keep a diary. You may want to set aside a month in which you note down every interaction that you have with members of your group (including when you pray for them). Note down thoughts and feelings, keep names to initials only. Make sure that you keep it in a safe place where no one else will see it—it's confidential. At the end of the month read back over the diary in the light of the subjects in this *Oasis* and reflect on how you go about the business of pastoring. What is really good and where do you need help to improve? This exercise can be made even more valuable by reflecting with a friend, minister, or spiritual director.

Flooded Out!

Within any group of Christian leaders there must be some mutual accountability for the way in which each person practises the art of pastoral care. After all, it affects the whole team (particularly if they run the group that feeds into yours!) Write each of the titles from this *Oasis* on to a separate sheet of paper. Split into pairs and give each pair one of the sheets (if you have fewer than twelve leaders then give everyone as many as is necessary). Ask people to come up with one sentence for their title which describes the way in which they think it should be offered within your ministry. The sentence should start with the words 'We are responsible to God, each other and those whom we serve for…' Try to be as clear and as simple as possible. For instance, you might want to say, 'Love: we are responsible to God and each other and those whom we serve for seeking to love all in the way that Jesus showed.' However, you will be able to come up with something much more specific and suited to your ministry. What you will end up with is a list that expresses something of the core values of your pastoral work. They could then become a regular focus for praying as a team and as a church for your work. In the long term, why not encourage people to pair up into prayer partnerships to support each other in growing towards these aims?

Spiritual growth: signs of life

Incredible! All you had done was to explain the Easter story using your new resource, talking to the children about Jesus coming back to life and being a special friend. You did not think you had done it particularly well and certainly the last-minute preparation did not help. But, during the craft activity, children talked to you quietly as they worked, about asking Jesus to step into their lives and become their special friend. By the end of the morning, three of them had made very clear statements about wanting to follow Jesus in their lives. You were ecstatic. This sort of thing never happened to you! You wonder what effect it might have on the rest of the group, and how Ally, a previously unresponsive child who influences others, could really turn the group around. Over the next few weeks you start a small group for children who want to know more and they enthusiastically explore what it means to be a Christian. Things are looking good and the children really seem to be growing. A few weeks later you get a telephone call from Ally's mum. Ally has been caught stealing from the local shop and, although she is only eight, the shopkeeper is making a real fuss. It soon becomes clear that this is not the first time. As you jump into the car your mind wanders back over the last few months and back to the Easter story. What did it mean for Ally to become a friend of God? Has she been telling you what you want to hear because she enjoys the group? What seemed so simple suddenly looks terribly complicated, and you wonder where God is in all this. As you pull up in front of the house, Ally's mum opens the door. You can see the tears starting to flow.

Understanding how children, young people and adults grow spiritually is vital if you are to avoid either having unrealistic expectations, or diluting the challenge of faith to a point where it is no longer Christianity. This *Oasis* considers some aspects of spiritual growth as they affect youth or children's ministry. As we look into the gospels and Paul's letters there will be both challenge and encouragement, so keep your ears and eyes open. But remember that as you look for spiritual growth in the lives of others the first question to ask is, 'Can I see any evidence of this growth in my own life?'

✳ The bigger picture   Mark 12:28–34

The most important one is this: 'Listen, Israel! The Lord our God is the only Lord. Love the Lord your God with all your heart, with all your soul, with all your mind, and with all your strength.' (Mark 12:29–30)

For many people, 'spiritual' suggests a greater breadth and personal meaningfulness, in contrast to the sometimes restrictive, formal or negative associations with 'religious'.
R. Nye, *Children, Spirituality and Religion*

Most adults spend a lot of time keeping their lives in a series of watertight compartments. The problems arise when things start to spill over from one area to another. In contrast, children find it difficult to compartmentalize. They move freely between different subjects and concepts that can seem, at times, almost random. Questions about religious faith can arise at any moment, sparked off by any event. They possess a natural interconnectedness that seems to disappear as they grow up. And it is to such a sense that Jesus points in his reply to the question from the young lawyer.

'What is the most important thing in the world?'

'Well,' replies Jesus, 'it is to love God with all that you are, in every situation, and to love those around you like you love yourself.'

The very Jewish expression of heart, soul, mind and strength encompasses all that constitutes our humanity. Too often we define Christian growth into narrow, culture-specific signs of religious duty: coming to church, praying out loud, agreeing with our teaching. All these things have value, but they can never be the sum total of Christian expression or development. The spiritual growth of children, as Rebecca Nye suggests, takes place in a wider context: the connectedness of their spiritual, emotional, physical and intellectual worlds. As these develop they affect one another, so a 'crisis of faith' may simply be the growing intellectual awareness of critical issues, and the dissatisfaction with church may be comparable to a blossoming of emotions associated with adolescence.

The spiritual growth of children and leaders is seen in all that we are: heart, soul, mind and strength.

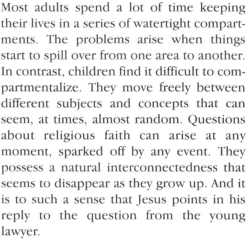

✳ Evidence of hunger   John 6:25–59

'I am the bread of life,' Jesus told them. 'Those who come to me will never be hungry; those who believe in me will never be thirsty … And I will raise them to life on the last day.' (John 6:35, 40)

He wants God very much; he is hungry and thirsty for God, and perhaps all that he is able to tell God is that he has a hunger and a thirst for him, though even that is very feeble, but he wishes that the hunger and thirst were more.
M. Ramsey, *Through the Year with Michael Ramsey*

We live in a society where images of satisfaction bombard us every day: TV cooking, ice-cream adverts and a whole host of other images present us with the desirability of physical satisfaction found in food. Images of hunger are often negative: the starving in Africa, malnourished children. The message is clear: it is not good to be hungry. But Jesus has a different view. A prerequisite of spiritual growth is to admit that we are hungry and in need of spiritual food. To grow up is to continue to recognize that need, which will be there for ever. The moment that we start to feel self-satisfied, no longer in need of God's sustenance, then we should worry. Jesus offers us the food that 'lasts for eternal life', because that food is none other than himself, 'the bread of life'. There is a promise of fulfilment and satisfaction that can only be found in God. Jesus had to point out to the people questioning him that it had always been God who had sustained them. Throughout the scriptures the attribute of hungering or thirsting for God is one that is commended. Such a hunger for Jesus is not one related to our physical needs, as Jesus pointed out to the excited crowd, nor one born out of emotional experience or psychological inadequacy, but rather from receiving and understanding the truth about Jesus. It is in coming to, and believing in, Jesus that we acknowledge and find satisfaction for hunger and thirst.

The spiritual growth of young people and leaders is seen in our hunger and thirst for the living God.

✻ Evidence of conflict   Ephesians 6

For we are not fighting against human beings but against the wicked spiritual forces in the heavenly world, the rulers, authorities, and cosmic powers of this dark age. (Ephesians 6:12)

Then Christian's sword flew out of his hand. 'Now,' said Apollyon, 'I am sure I have you,' and he almost beat him to death. But, as God would have it, as Apollyon gave his final blows to finish him off, Christian's hand touched his sword, which gave him fresh spirit. He gripped his sword with all his might and said, 'Rejoice not against me, O my enemy: when I fall, I shall rise again,' giving Apollyon a deadly thrust which caused him to fall back as if mortally wounded. Summoning all his strength, Christian rose to his feet and advanced towards him, crying, 'In all these things we are more than conquerors through him that loved us.' This was too much for Apollyon; he spread his wings and flew away.

John Bunyan, *The Pilgrim's Progress*

Who gives you more cause for concern? The child who listens attentively and never has a problem with your teaching, or the young person who always seems to be in conflict with Christian standards, who finds it hard to relate them to normal life? Setting aside the possibility of bad teaching, different sociological backgrounds or particular psychological types, we often cope better with conformists. But is that necessarily right? As he enters the valleys of humility and death, Christian, Bunyan's allegorical traveller in faith, meets Apollyon and engages him. The resonance with Ephesians 6 is clear. Paul, having explained how Jesus creates a new society where barriers are broken down and where people are reconciled and redeemed, confronts the reality of evil and shows the way in which Christians are called to face it. The picture of the armour of God is slightly better known than the purpose for which it is given, explained in verses 10–13. But understanding the purpose is crucial: it is so that we will not just survive, but succeed, to 'still hold your ground'. In our modern translations the word 'finally' might lead us to think that Paul is talking about some end-of-the-world apocalyptic event. However, this is better understood as 'for the remaining time'. So for Christians there is a constant battle against both personal supernatural powers and the more structural 'powers' that can be agents of evil in society.

The spiritual growth of children and leaders is seen in the signs of battle, as faith and reality engage and progress is made.

✳ Being: the growing character
Galatians 5:16–25

And those who belong to Christ Jesus have put to death their human nature with all its passions and desires. The Spirit has given us life; he must also control our lives. (Galatians 5:24–25)

> *Father, when we drink from your Spirit our lives change.*
> *Help me today to come to the living water:*
> *then grow your fruit in me. Amen.*

Tim Mayfield, *The Spirit of Jesus*

For some years the list of fruits of the Spirit in Galatians 5 depressed me! It just seemed like a list of unattainable expectations, a picture of the perfect Christian. However, as time has gone on I think I have begun to understand a little of what Paul is trying to say. The question facing the church in Galatia was, 'What relevance does the Jewish law have for Gentile Christians?' Paul has addressed this topic all through the letter by pointing to the evidence of the Holy Spirit in their lives as proof that they need not rely on the law. He does not condemn the law but asserts that the Spirit fulfils its requirements. The solution to Paul's dilemma, outlined in verses 16–21, is that those who belong to Christ Jesus have put to death their human nature. It sounds as though we suddenly became perfect when we became a Christian. But note that it is *we* who have to do the 'putting to death'. The call of Jesus is to take up our cross daily and follow him, to continually take this attitude of crucifying our sin, that the Spirit might work God's character in us. Our continued problems are often exacerbated when we refuse to recognize or practise this truth. This 'putting to death' is to be done in God's strength: it's in partnership, only made possible by God. As we obey God and allow 'the Spirit to control our desires', we enter into an active following in faith of what the Spirit requires; hence the list in earlier verses, the evidence of spiritual growth.

The spiritual growth of young people and leaders is seen in lives actively engaged in trying to keep in step with God.

47

✳ Doing: the changed actions   James 1:22 – 25

Do not deceive yourselves by just listening to his word; instead, put it into practice. (James 1:22)

But not only faith, perfect and in every way complete, but all right knowledge of God is born of obedience. And surely in this respect God has, by his singular providence, taken thought for mortals through all ages.

Calvin, *Institutes II.6.2*

Watching children or young people grow immerses one in the observation of change: physical, emotional, spiritual and intellectual. Such wide-ranging, rapid growth can make the Christian call to a changed life somewhat perplexing. To demand change prematurely might just be stepping on the creativity and freedom that are so vital to healthy development. Add to the mix the desire of each generation to conform the next to their own cultural expectations and it is easy to see why some are wary of asking children and young people to change their lifestyle. Building on Jesus' teaching, James stresses that professed faith and practical action are intrinsically linked. They are two sides of the same coin. It is by God's grace through faith that we're reconciled to God, and our changed actions are evidence of our professed faith. True evidence of understanding is seen in our willingness to change our actions to be more like Jesus. In his landmark work, *Institutes of The Christian Religion*, John Calvin starts by outlining his convictions about how human people can have 'knowledge of God the creator'. Although his eyes are firmly fixed on the need for faith, he constantly makes the link between faith and obedience, from which 'all right knowledge of God is born, encouraging us to be those who 'apply themselves teachably to God's word'. The outworking of this for youth and children's leaders must surely be to keep faith and actions firmly linked together. However, actions, for us and our young people, should be appropriate to the culture and age of each person. In the search to understand what true obedience means today, we need to spend prayerful moments filtering out our own culture and expectations in our advice and expectations of others. For instance, to expect the thirteen-year-old boy with a breaking voice to sing confidently in his peer group may well be asking for an inappropriate response! More seriously, when challenging people to change, we need to consider the whole person whom God has brought to that particular stage of life; otherwise we may simply be leading them towards the deception of which James speaks, as we ask the impossible.

The spiritual growth of children and leaders is seen in appropriate changed actions.

✳ Giving: the results of receiving

1 Corinthians 12

There are different kinds of spiritual gifts, but the same Spirit gives them... Since you are eager to have the gifts of the Spirit, you must try above everything else to make greater use of those which help to build up the church. (1 Corinthians 12:4; 14:12)

Let us not adopt an understanding of spiritual gifts which effectively excludes a God who transcends our finite minds, and who in his love reveals himself unexpectedly in our mortal existence.

D. Prior, *The Message of 1 Corinthians*

Disagreements over spiritual gifts have caused the rising and falling of whole denominations. Amidst the wealth of different opinions a few things are clear from 1 Corinthians. The problem in the church was lack of love in the use of gifts. Paul's famous chapter 13 is written to encourage that quality of love to be present amongst members of the church, as God gives and enables the use of spiritual gifts. Paul's thrust is that tongues, healing, prophecy, knowledge, hospitality, administration, service, miracles, teaching and all the other gifts should be offered in the context of love and should 'build up the church'. What gifts do you have for this purpose? Perhaps the extreme stances taken by many denominations, and our own patronizing attitudes to children and young people, have resulted in the lack of teaching and practice of such things in youth or children's ministry. It seems that they have been placed in a 'theological danger zone' which we don't quite understand, and find all a bit too scary. But God's gifts are still there for building up his people and empowering them for mission. The original language conveys the sense of birthday presents, to be enjoyed and celebrated, given out of love. We may not understand them, we may find them scary, but to ignore them may be, as David Prior suggests, actually limiting God because we cannot control him. Equally an undiscerning approach leads to the problems experienced by the Corinthian church who exercised little control and failed to build themselves up. Perhaps, if we begin to explore this area with our children and young people, it will be *us* who are built up as *they* exercise God's good gifts.

The spiritual growth of young people and leaders is seen through their receipt and use of spiritual gifts.

Taking the Plunge

1. How does the response of the young lawyer in Mark 12:32 and 33 differ from what Jesus says in verses 29–31? Is the difference important? How do you encourage yourself and the age-group with which you work to love God with heart, soul, mind and strength?
2. What does Jesus say it means to feed on the bread of life? (Look at verses 29, 35.) What sort of satisfaction does Jesus offer? (Look at verses 37, 39–40, 51, 54–58.) What evidence of hunger is there in (a) your own life, (b) your church, (c) your work with children and young people?
3. In Ephesians 6:10–13 what is the relationship between us and God? Think of one child or young person you know. Is there any evidence of spiritual conflict in their life?
4. What does Paul advise those who want to grow a Christian life? (Look at Galatians 5:16, 24, 25.) What do you think Paul is suggesting: (a) that we live good lives and so find the Spirit of God? or (b) that we follow the Spirit who

will naturally produce godly lives in us?

5. What actions do you normally associate with spiritual growth? Are any of these really just your own cultural assumptions?

6. What place do spiritual gifts have within your own life and also your work with children or young people?

Soaking In

For this exercise you will need to find a small houseplant. Read through John 15:1–18, part of the 'farewell discourses' spoken by Jesus around the time of his arrest and trial. The claim to be the true vine is the last of the well-known 'I am' sayings found in John's Gospel. The image would not have been lost on his Jewish audience; it adorned the gate to the temple, which may have been visible to the group as they moved from the upper room across the Kidron valley. Jesus had already used the image when publicly speaking of God's judgment on Israel (Mark 12:1–2) and now applies it to himself. Read the passage again and pause at verses 4 and 10 to look at your plant. Look at how the whole plant fits together, how leaves rely on their stems, which in turn rely on the main stalk. Think about how your plant illustrates the relationship of Jesus and God: what actions does God have to take for the good of the whole (vv. 2, 6)? How do God's actions explain the defection of Judas, to which the passage also refers? How does growth occur (4–5, 7–10ff.)? What's the purpose of the whole process (vv. 8, 16) ? Write down your thoughts as you go, and then apply them to yourself and your ministry.

Overflow

To remind yourself to keep on looking for and praying towards spiritual growth, why not plant a seedling? Find something that grows easily in a pot—this is about prayer, not gardening! Put the seedling somewhere suitable and where you can see it regularly. You could tape a copy of John 15:8 on to the pot as a reminder. As the plant grows, take time to pray through your group and for their spiritual growth. Each stage of the plant may prompt different

thoughts: shoots from barren soil, healthy growth, pruning. As you see the physical growth give thanks to God for the spiritual growth in your members that, as John reminds us, is a source and occasion for great joy.

Flooded Out!

From time to time those who lead children or young people need to look at what they do as a team and assess how it helps or hinders spiritual growth. This is not to constrict God, but rather to note what seems to be helpful.

Draw on a sheet of blank paper two graph axes and copy enough for your team. The horizontal axis represents time, and the vertical spiritual growth. Ask each team member to focus on a person in their age group whom they know well, and plot what they know of their spiritual growth over the past year. As they mark the highs and lows they should write in useful comments about causes, problems and solutions. When finished, pair leaders up and get them to compare graphs. After a short while present the group with the following questions:

• *Is there anything in what we currently do that really seems to help people grow in their Christian life?*
• *Of the rest of our programme, what must we definitely continue to do and why?*
• *What should we stop doing to give more time to the work that produces fruit?*

This exercise is best done if leaders have used some of the 'Testing the Water' material from this *Oasis* beforehand.

The team

You're late! Time seems to rush by, what with the kids to get ready and the house to tidy for your parents who had to choose this Sunday to come and visit. As time ticks away, the tension rises, sharp words are exchanged, and before you know it you have two minutes before you are supposed to be leading the session at church. You pile into the car and set off. Abandoning the family in the car-park you rush into the hall, only to find that everything has started. Your heart drops as a sense of failure overwhelms you. Then Jim, one of your helpers, gently takes you into a corner.

'It's OK, don't panic,' he whispers, 'Jodi is doing the story, and we've sorted the other activities. I've arranged for Brian to come over from church and play for the songs at about quarter-to, and all the craft stuff is laid out next door. Relax. Things are OK.'

You're not sure whether to cry, or leap in the air for joy. At last the team really seems to know that it's a team, not just a group of people who happen to have a common interest. At the end of the session as you clear away you find it hard to know how to say thanks. However, the rest of the team are genuinely interested and make it easy for you to offload your stress. Now lunch with your parents seems possible, even likeable!

For as many good experiences that we have of teams working well, there are probably many more examples of teams that work badly. Lack of commitment, unreliability, mistrust, jealousy, pride and a whole host of other factors can conspire against a successful team. But God has made us part of a team, a family, a church which needs all the different parts to function together. One look at ministry in the Bible and you soon discover that there is no space for the 'one man (or woman) band'. Whatever your situation, you are in a team—even if it's just you and the vicar. So in this *Oasis* we will be thinking about the team as being part of the context in which work with children and young people takes place. It's not the last word on the subject, but an exploration of some basics. Investing in teamwork is an investment for the whole of the ministry so that all can experience the joy and blessing that flow from a team that really works.

Testing the Water

✳ The team: the place where prayer is the priority   Philippians 1:1–11

From Paul and Timothy, servants of Christ Jesus—To all God's people in Philippi... I thank God for you every time I think of you; and every time I pray for you all, I pray with joy... (Philippians 1:1–4)

More things are wrought by prayer than this world dreams of.
Alfred, Lord Tennyson, *Idylls of the King*

Most of us know that we don't pray together enough for the ministry in which we are involved. One of the joys of reading Paul's letters was that he prayed for those continuing his work at a distance. I mean, he really prayed for them. He had a vision of what prayer could achieve that goes far beyond taking away headaches and making children happier, important as those occasionally are. As he writes to the church in Philippi, look at his opening words. He thanks God for them and makes it clear that they are regularly on his mind; he prays for them with joy because he has learned to see what God is doing in their lives. But there is more. Look on to verse 9: he prays for a 'growing love', a 'true knowledge', and a 'perfect judgment'. And if that all seems a bit too much like wishful thinking, he claims that the results of such praying will be that they will be free from 'impurity' and 'blame', and that their lives will be filled with 'good qualities', bringing glory to God. When did you last pray like that for your children and young people? This prayer was one of faith and vision. Paul's understanding was that, because Jesus is Lord, prayer engages with God and as such is filled with the faith and vision of God himself.

No matter what sort of team God has given you, we are all called to pray like this. If your ministry has gone off the boil, if the team feels awkward and dry, the chances are that somewhere along the line you have stopped, or not started, praying like this. So allow your mind to be changed, and begin to be a team that takes prayer seriously. Why not make the first half of every meeting a time of prayer, leave the 'business' to the second part, and see what God does amongst you!

✳ The team: the place where leaders are trained   2 Timothy 1:1–18

To Timothy my dear son: May God the Father and Christ Jesus our Lord give you grace, mercy and peace... Hold firmly to the true words that I taught you,

53

as the example for you to follow, and remain in the faith and love that are ours in union with Christ Jesus (2 Timothy 1:2, 13)

If you want to become a person who brings out the best in others, focus on their futures and look at them through the eyes of faith.

R. Johnston, *Developing Student Leaders*

My teenage years were full of dreams of flying fast jets for the Royal Air Force, and for a while that was exactly what I trained to do. But that was before I met someone called Mike. Mike asked me to come and help out on a summer camp for 8–12 year-olds. What started as a Christian camp developed into a serious vocation, and eventually to full-time ministry. I can't remember much of what Mike said but I can see what he did, for me and others. He looked at people with an eye to their future. Mike would probably not call himself a trainer, or necessarily have recognized our relationship as a formal mentorship. Nevertheless I heard from Mike, as Timothy did from Paul, 'true words', and I saw in Mike, as Timothy did in Paul, 'an example for me to follow'. I don't think Mike even knew what the future would hold, he just seemed to know that with God it had endless possibilities.

The relationship between Paul and Timothy is just one amongst many 'mentor'-style relationships in the Bible. Jesus himself taught, showed, enabled and empowered the disciples to follow in his footsteps and reproduce his ministry. Things have now come full circle: I can begin to see people who have been drawn into ministry by what God has done through me. The joy of mentoring others is that it is a two-way process where as much is received as is given; and, with fresh ideas and perspectives brought in, stagnation and sterility are avoided. Such a process is not the result of a degree course. It starts with ordinary leaders, selecting the most unlikely people, often in the gentlest of ways. But it is at the heart of a biblical pattern of ministry, so if God is for it, who can stand against it?

✳ The team: the place where conflict is dealt with   Philippians 4:1–3

Euodia and Syntyche, please, I beg you, try to agree as sisters in the Lord. (Philippians 4:2)

Some of the most talented people are terrible leaders because they have a crippling need to be loved by everyone.

James Schorr, *Bringing Out the Best in People*

The inability, or unwillingness, to deal with conflict is one of the most common failures in Christian ministry, crippling churches and groups. We are not told much about the situation to which Paul addresses himself in Philippians 4, other than the fact that there was division. However, such things are acknowledged in the scriptures as happening in ministry. So the first pointer towards conflict resolution becomes clear: we must acknowledge that it is happening and bring it into the open. Where conflicts lie dormant they fester and grow, acting like a cancer that gradually becomes fatal to the whole ministry.

The second pointer to a way forward is to realize our situation as Christians. The key is in understanding, as Paul reminded the Philippians, that we are 'in the Lord'. We are 'fellow workers, whose names are in God's book of the living'. We are not separate entities who have to exert personal rights and power to gain self-worth and acceptance. Paul's greeting in verse 1 makes clear the sort of relationship that we have with those who are 'in Christ'. So personal disagreements and disunity are a contradiction to what we have become in Christ. We need to be clear: disagreements will happen within any team, Christian ministry is no protection. But the difference is in how we handle them. Because we are secure in Christ, with our names written in God's book, we need not defend our fragile egos by sticking to our guns, claiming that we are on the side of right and truth—even if that is actually the case! The imperative is to confront the issue and seek to be the first to make an initiative towards reconciliation, even if that means humility and rejection. In that process of reconciliation we are making the good news of Christ concrete in our life together as a team. Through honesty, confrontation and reconciliation, joy is found as God demonstrates in us what it means to be in union, together, in Christ.

✳ The team: the place where all are accountable   Ephesians 4:1–16

Instead, by speaking the truth in a spirit of love, we must grow up in every way to Christ, who is the head. (Ephesians 4:15)

We have a vision of a Church in which those who work with young people are of a high calibre, and are valued and affirmed by the church and offered a framework of training, accountability and support.

General Synod Board of Education, *Youth A Part: Young People and the Church*

I am sure you know the story about the little boy who had the courage to point out that the emperor had no clothes. Many teams of Christian workers operate a collective culture of denying reality. Perhaps we put off acknowledging or confronting differences because we don't know how to deal with them. But as the church in Ephesus needed to hear, so do we: that we are called to speak the truth in a spirit of love (in this case against false teaching). Paul sees mutual accountability built into the church because people previously separated by human barriers are now one—a condition made possible because Christ has 'brought us peace', by 'breaking down the wall that separated' people. Division and error deny what Christ did on the cross. So we are called to 'speak the truth in love' one to another so that all

can 'grow up into Christ who is the head'. Such thinking needs to become part of the culture of every team. Disagreements are no longer the criticism of those competing for glory, but rather stem from the love of those seeking to serve one another. And this accountability is not just in speech, but also refers to notions of maintaining, living and doing the truth, but always in the context of love. A team that wants to grow and mature will aim to make speaking the truth in love a high priority amongst its members.

✳ The team: the place where gifts are valued

Acts 6:1–7

So the twelve apostles called the whole group of believers together and said, 'It is not right for us to neglect the preaching of God's word in order to handle finances. So then, brothers and sisters, choose seven men among you who are known to be full of the Holy Spirit and wisdom, and we will put them in charge of this matter.' (Acts 6:2–3)

Success in a team depends not only on having the right people in each functional role, but also on correctly identifying their team roles—and applying this knowledge.

G. and R. Jones, *Teamwork*

I doubt if there has ever been a worse game of football than the one I played in when I was ten. I was very proud to be the goalkeeper of the school's second team. However, by the time half-time came we appeared to be six-nil down. As we came off the pitch the whole team made for me and started to berate me for letting so many in. I could not understand what they were complaining about. After all, I had not let the ball touch the net, and that was how you scored a goal. So I thought! Needless to say, that was my last game for that team. Actually it was about my last game of football ever. I was in the wrong role, in the wrong team and, I suspect, in the wrong game.

A team that does not identify, deploy and encourage its members' gifts correctly will never function effectively. The result will be unhappiness, lack of vision, feelings of inadequacy and ineffective ministry. As the Christian church grew and changed, so different situations required the use of gifts and abilities to change. Although not written as a manual in team development, the principle in Acts 6 is still clear: different people are called to different ministries. The church recognized and ordered its leadership to enable their gifts and callings to be properly deployed. We also perform different roles within the team, and we need to get both right if we are to hope for success. If you follow the story of Acts through, it is clear that individuals need to be in the right role, so that the whole church can move forward in its core task of mission.

Fortunately for the world of football I soon realized that I was indeed in the wrong game. In ministry we should regularly evaluate and adjust our roles within the team to suit changed circumstances and personal development. Taking time to do that provides a point of refocus and refreshment, because to be God's person in God's place, at God's time, is to truly be blessed.

✳ The team: the place where unity is prized

Psalm 133

How wonderful it is, how pleasant, for God's people to live together in harmony! (Psalm 133:1)

Our unity is in Him, our separations are in ourselves. As we attain to one-ness with Him, so we shall attain to union with one another in Him.

Father Andrew SDC, *Meditations for Every Day*

'Why is it,' asked ten-year-old Peter as we walked across the field, 'that all you leaders like each other so much? You must spend a lot of time together at home.'

'Actually, we have never met before this week,' I said.

He looked at me quizzically. 'But why do you get on so well?'

The discussion continued, but what struck home was the fact that Peter had sensed unity in a team of very different people who had never worked together before. That unity had struck him as being strange, something other than his normal experience, and it led, as we continued to walk, into a chat about God and what he could do for people.

In Psalm 133 we find a striking picture of unity. In Israel all the people were considered as brothers and sisters to each other, so this unity extends beyond the family into society. Lurking behind this psalm may be the ordination rituals of Exodus 29:21, where the oil, mixed with blood, was sprinkled on the priest to make him holy. Could it be that this 'echo' from Israel's history tells us that unity is not just nice or pleasing but is in some way a sign of holiness. Godly unity is holy unity. The oil that was used would also have been fragrant, conveying the idea that unity is good to have and has an effect beyond its immediate participants. Imagine what it might feel like to be the recipient of such an anointing—perhaps a little embarrassing at first, but surely ultimately a joyful and pleasant experience. In the New Testament we discover that unity is to be found in Jesus and in his truth, so our common commitment to him brings blessing. My discussion with Peter illustrated the effects of unity: our commitment to each other on the team had overflowed into his life, causing him to ask questions. Such unity is given from God (note the emphasis in the psalm on things 'running down' and 'falling') and made concrete in our actions: not speaking ill of other team members, serving each other, backing each other up, refusing to be drawn into divisive arguments.

How much Christian ministry is sucked dry of joy and blessing because we refuse to make concrete the unity that we have in Christ? For a team that makes such unity concrete in thought, word, and action is the team where the Lord has promised his blessing—'life that never ends'.

Taking the Plunge

1. Why is Paul able to pray in the way that he does? (Look at Philippians 1:6.) What concerns Paul more, the physical or spiritual needs of the Philippians? What can your team learn about praying for your children and young people from this?

2. What is Paul's priority in his mentoring relationship with Timothy? (Look at 2 Timothy 1:3–4.) What areas of Timothy's life is Paul interested in? Out of all the advice he gives in verses 1–18, what principles of mentoring can still apply to us?

3. What part are you playing in helping to resolve conflict in your team? What principles from Philippians 4:1–3 and Matthew 18:15–17 have you yet to apply to the situation?

4. What should be the hallmarks of Christian accountability? (Look at Ephesians 4:1–2, 12, 15.) How, and to whom, is your work with children and young people accountable?

5. Can Acts 6:1–8 tell us anything about how ministry should be organized? What are your primary gifts and how are they deployed within your team?

6. What words are used in Psalm 133 to describe unity? How do you try to build unity and togetherness in your team?

Soaking In

For this exercise you will need two sheets of paper (one headed 'Thanks', the other 'Ideas'), a pen and a Bible. As you read through Psalm 133 focus in on the four descriptive words: 'wonderful', 'pleasant', 'harmony', 'blessing'. It may be helpful to picture the celebration as the priest was anointed for his office or perhaps the 'feel' of the words is more important, conveying their own meanings to you. Now choose one of the issues from 'Testing the Water': prayer, accountability, conflict, gifts, training/mentoring or unity. You may want to note down the appropriate Bible passages and read them again. As you think about each one, ask yourself, 'What is there about this issue that is wonderful, pleasant, that builds harmony, or is a blessing?' As you reflect on your situation in the light of the biblical principles, write down what comes to mind on your sheets of paper: things to thank God for, and ideas to work on. If you have time you could move on to another aspect of teamwork. Put the sheet of things to 'thank God for' somewhere where you will see it often (Bible, fridge, back of the toilet door!) Then you can continue to give thanks for those things. The sheet of ideas to work on may form some priorities for your team to consider.

Overflow

Look at the picture of the swimming pool opposite and imagine it is an illustration of your team of youth and children's workers. Try to place the following:
* *where you fit into the team at present;*
* *where you think you ought to be in the team;*
* *where your team leader might be;*
* *which person best illustrates your team's attitude towards: (a) training, (b) gifts, (c) accountability, (d) conflict, (e) prayer, (f) unity.*

This exercise may help you set some personal priorities for how you fit into the team but it is also beneficial if done by the whole team together.

Flooded Out!

About once a year every team needs to stop and check how they're doing. You could use the swimming pool picture described in the 'Overflow' section, or the Bible study in 'Soaking In'. It might be helpful to assign a different subject to individuals or pairs before the meeting so that you can spend the maximum time identifying what is good and what needs to develop.

   As one way of building your team you could play the 'Build a Path' game on page 60.

Build a Path

Write each statement below on to one card (record or blank visiting cards would be ideal) and hand them out to your team members so that everyone has at least one. There are 33 cards, so you may need to give more than one to each person, or share. This does not matter.

Team members must not show their cards to anyone else. Working together ask your team to work out when the path is completed. Time them. This can be done in 12 minutes, so stop them after about 25 minutes. The correct answer is 8 June. It is best if they work out a calendar and the calculate from this when each stage is completed. Suggest this if they get stuck.

At the end, debrief. Find out about their feelings. Make comments on people's attitudes: who joined in and who did not. Make the point that every card was vital and therefore every person's contribution was crucial if the answer was to be found out. Ask what happened when people opted out.

Ask your team how the team worked during the exercise, what were the good points, what were the bad. Decide on some of the things your team needs to give thanks for and also one thing that you need to work on. Now pray about them.

All concrete and tools are delivered on Thursday 4 April.

Today is Monday 1 April.

The path is 100 metres long.

It takes four people to lay the path. No work can be done if only three people are present.

Peter is ill on Sunday 12 May and can't help lay the path on that day.

Hard core can't be delivered until Wednesday 24 April.

It rains on Friday 3 May.

Peter has to go to a wedding all day on Saturday 20 April.

Four men work ten hours a day on the path.

It rains on Saturday 18 May.

Peter is ill on Sunday 26 May and can't gelp lay the path.

No work on the path can be done either on the day when it rains, or on the day after it rains.

It rains on Friday 17 May.

The path is made of concrete with a hard core foundation.

John has ample money to buy supplies.

Derek can only work on the path for three weekends a month (any three weekends).

John can only work on the path at weekends.

Peter can work on the path at any time.

Work can start as soon as everyone is available.

Ian can work on the path at any time.

John, Peter, Derek and Ian are all good friends living in the same town, and except where stated can be quickly and easlity available to lay the path.

The only people who work on the path are John, Peter, Derek and Ian.

The path is laid in three stages—(1) preparation of the ground (2) hard core foundation (3) concrete top layer.

It takes two men five hours to lay ten metres of hard core.

The four men work in pairs on the hard core foundation.

All the hard core foundation has to be complete before any concrete is laid.

Once the hard core is finished, the men take the rest of the day off.

It takes the four men all working together two hours to prepare five metres of ground for the path.

All the preparation of the ground has to be complete before the hard core foundation is laid.

All four men must work together to lay the concrete.

It takes the men five hours to lay ten metres of concrete.

All the ground has to be prepared before the path is laid. All the hard core has to be laid before any concrete can be put down.

John is wanting to build a path. He needs three friends to help him.

OASIS 8

Plugging In...

The church

It had taken all of your skill and effort to get the teenagers to come to the all-age worship event. As you stand nervously at the back of church waiting for it to begin, you hope that it is going to be worth all the effort. Suddenly, the vicar stands and starts the welcome.

'Good morning everyone,' she says in a bright, 'isn't-the-world-lovely' sort of voice. 'How nice it is to see you all this morning. And a very special welcome to members of the Rock who have joined us this morning.'

You can see some of the group beginning to snarl, as only teenagers can. Thankfully the first song about trees, flowers and small furry animals starts up before they have the chance to get lippy. The rest of the event treads a fine line between reasonable and downright patronizing. Even your own six-year-old was bored and left out. Well, you think, at least I made the effort. A few days later you meet with the other youth and children's leaders for your yearly get-together. To your surprise you begin to hear them saying exactly the same sort of thing about the all-age worship session. In short, it seemed to please no one at all. You make a mental note to pop in and see the vicar before all the criticism finds its target, it can't be an easy job. But it is clear that St Puddleswades-in-the-Thicket needs to think seriously about how all the people relate to each other. The issue is wider than just all-age worship, and it certainly is no one person's fault. As you leave the meeting behind and walk home through the cold night air, you begin to wonder if there is any hope for either the church, or the younger generation. Are they really irreconcilable?

One of the most pressing issues faced by youth and children's leaders is the relationship of their ministries to the local church. Whilst some counsel a separation of church-based and outreach work, and others suggest that anything that is not explicitly church-based must be stopped, most ordinary leaders struggle on, doing all that they can. Instead of recommending one or the other, we shall take a step back and look again at what the church is, could be, should be and might become. When we begin to get God's vision, we might know where best to start. So in this *Oasis* we are going to look again at what sort of church God is creating, what its purpose is, and what some of its characteristics should be. Allow yourself to be amazed, astounded, humbled, excited and envisioned, because there is indeed hope, for those who have the eyes to see it.

✳ A sign of the gospel Ephesians 2:11–22

By his death on the cross Christ destroyed their enmity; by means of the cross he united both races into one body and brought them back to God. (Ephesians 2:16)

How is it possible that the gospel should be credible, that people should come to believe that the power which has the last word on human affairs is represented by a man hanging on a cross? ...the only answer, the only hermeneutic of the gospel, is a congregation of men and women who believe it and live by it.

Lesslie Newbigin, *The Gospel in a Pluralist Society*

Hermeneutic. It's one of those words that sounds like a nasty experience in hospital. But it's really rather simple, and a lot less painful. It refers to how we interpret something, how we understand it. Biblical hermeneutics is really all about how we interpret and understand what the Bible says to us today. So read again what Lesslie Newbigin has to say about the church, and then take a deep breath! The only way that people are going to *understand* Christianity is by seeing belief lived out by ordinary people. That is where Paul is headed in Ephesians chapter 2 as he explains what the church is all about. In his death Jesus made peace between people, in this case between Jews and Gentiles, so that now they are one body, with no division. So what will children and young people understand, from your church's example, about what the death of Jesus achieved for the church? Will they see one body, with no divisions, or will the picture presented be somewhat different? It is in relationship, in the church, that the unity Christ brings will be understood. It is not just one model of ministry, but the supreme route through which the truth of the cross is to be seen and believed. This should not be taken as evidence for depression as we give up on our church ever being able to change. But rather, a vision of what is possible when we allow God to change each one of us. God has given to each gathering of Christians the potential to be a life-changing force, simply by their existence. So one of the key purposes of the church is to become a sign of the gospel.

✳ Fellow-citizens Ephesians 2:11–22

So then, you Gentiles are not foreigners or strangers any longer; you are now fellow-citizens with God's people and members of the family of God. ...you too are being built together with all the others into a place where God lives through his Spirit. (Ephesians 2:19, 22)

It is [equally] obvious that Jesus calls individuals, not to stay in isolation, but to join the new community of God's people.

David Watson, *Discipleship*

Junior church, Sunday School, Youth Fellowship, Church of Tomorrow... we have all sorts of different ways of referring to the groups and activities that concern children and young people. Most of these terms set groups apart from that which we have come to call 'church', but which actually refers to Sunday morning adult worship. But when Paul talks to two groups within the church at Ephesus he does not call one of them 'church' and demand that the other joins in. Rather, he calls them *both* 'fellow-citizens with God's people and members of God's family'. There are no intergenerational distinctions; all are equal in God's sight, all are fellow-citizens. How much do we as leaders actually see our groups of young believers as church and how much are they seen as something other than church?

It has been suggested that we stop calling any one group or activity, including adult Sunday worship, 'church' and simply use the term to cover all the different activities of the local congregation. And it is amongst all of these faithful believers of every age that God lives through his Spirit. So we know that amongst the children and young people with whom we work there will be the church of today, not tomorrow. In fact, there will also be some leaders of the church today and tomorrow, if only we would take time aside to help and grow them. Whilst it is easy to criticize the church, we need the vision to see it as God sees it if we are to understand how to encourage our children and young people to relate to it. It is a community of fellow-citizens, a family of God, built on Jesus and inhabited by God himself.

✴ An organic body   Romans 12:1–8

In the same way, though we are many, we are one body in union with Christ, and we are all joined to each other as different parts of one body.
(Romans 12:5)

Dear God, Why did you make so many people? Could you make an-other earth and put the extras there?
J.B.

Marshall and Hample, *Children's Letters to God*

J.B.'s letter is quite understandable. We have all had times when we wish that we could select some of the spare people to be transported to God's other earth. In fact, I'm sure that you have a list ready right now! But to do so would miss out on a vital aspect of what it means to be church. The well-known image of the body speaks not only of different parts but also of an *organic* connection between those parts. That means that all the parts of God's church, the fellow-citizens, family members, are connected organically to each other. So the removal, or absence, of

any one part is not just sad or inconvenient; it is damaging and potentially life-threatening to the whole. Good practice in youth and children's ministry understands this organic link between different parts of the church and seeks ways in which that connection can be made concrete in the relationships and activity of the different members. Leaders recognize that it is their own Christian life that will suffer if the young people with whom they work are not part of church life. Although they may not feel it, the teenagers are actually suffering if the five-year-olds are excluded in some way. The over-sixties will be spiritually impoverished if their connection to younger people is not maintained. This intergenerational invisibility shows the truth of the gospel and the reality of what the church really is. A fragmented church is a church which denies the sort of church that Jesus established. But if we have the courage, vision and imagination to try to live out what it means to be the body of Christ, then we will begin to know and experience the church as Christ intended.

✳ A distinct community   1 Peter 2:9–12

But you are the chosen race, the King's priests, the holy nation, God's own people, chosen to proclaim the wonderful acts of God, who called you out of darkness into his own marvellous light. (1 Peter 2:9)

The church has a completely new task on its plate. We need to preach life, excitement for life, vision, passion, praise, celebration. Our human and planetary self-image needs rebuilding… we need to form communities where people are built up, encouraged and strengthened.

Be Real, a UK alternative worship community
http://www.maths.not.ac.uk/personal/mck/info.html

I wonder if you have ever played 'spot the difference'. You know, the sort of game where there are two pictures that have minor differences. A small line here, a missing eye there and before you know it you have completed the competition, filled in the sentence and are hoping for a share in £1,000,000! In contrast to the rather easy competitions on paper, it can be increasingly difficult to spot the difference between the church and the society. I once worked in a church where we were all challenged as to the differences between ourselves and the society around us. In fact, apart from our beliefs, we discovered few observable differences. It was not that we were trying to go on a hairshirt-beating guilt trip. The sad fact was that our faith did not seem significantly to impact the sort of house we bought, the cars we drove or the goods we purchased.

However, the fact is that a change *has* taken place. Christians have been brought from darkness into God's light. That means, as Peter goes on to explain, that we are now strangers and aliens in this world, because we are fellow-citizens of the kingdom of God. What we should be aiming for is a sort of 'spot the similarities' competition where our faith makes every difference to our life and what we do with it. One of the interesting developments of many alternative worship initiatives is a return to this physical community of committed relationships where people can celebrate life, vision, and passion. If we have the courage to do that, then there will be a place where children and young people, and the rest of the church, can find common space as they realize what it means to be strangers and aliens together, called into God's marvellous light.

✳ A special place   John 6:53–58

Those who eat my flesh and drink my blood live in me, and I live in them. (John 6:56)

In the sacrament of the Eucharist we are bringing into the present everything that speaks of what God once did in Jesus Christ: the incarnation, the suffering and the cross, the presence of Christ after his resurrection, the giving of the Holy Spirit, because they are not trapped like flies in the aspic of time.

M. Mayne, *This Sunrise of Wonder*

In most churches, whatever their tradition, communion is a special time. Many people use special words, not used at other times; we have special things, cups and plates, wine, bread or wafers; and in some Christian communities there are special clothes, colours and smells. The sense of 'specialness' is one thing that marks out communion from all other times in church life. Although the exact understanding of communion has been the source of some of the deepest divisions in the church, most Christians, whether they emphasize the memory of Jesus' death or the action of God upon bread and wine, are agreed both that we should think about Jesus' life and death and that in some way Christ is particularly present. It is a special time, for God's special people.

However, these things are often left behind in both our ministries and our lives, yet they are still part of our own experience and the collective life of our fath community. Obviously, every church has different policies regarding children and communion and these must be respected, but perhaps there is a way in which this special meal could impact the younger members of God's special people.

To weave some of this 'specialness' into our ministry may be to start by using colour, light, signs and symbols within our groups. It may be simply to bring along some of the special things that we use in church—cups, plates, bread and wine. These things are the living memories of our faith which remind us that what happened all those years ago is not 'trapped in the aspic of time' in a foreign land, but rather is part of what it means to be Christian today.

✳ An agent of mission   Luke 10:1–12

After this the Lord chose another seventy-two men and sent them out two by two, to go ahead of him to every town and place where he himself was about to go... Go! I am sending you like lambs among wolves. (Luke 10:1, 3)

There will be no future for the broad Church in a post-modern world. We will have to return to structures... akin to the monastery, the religious community and the sect.

Andrew Walker, *Telling the Story*

If you could recreate the church from scratch I wonder what it would look like? Have a go with your leaders or young people sometime. It will, no doubt, look very different from what we have now, and that may not be a bad thing! Over time it's easy to lose sight of the objectives and reasons for the church. You will have noticed that in this *Oasis* we have not talked about buildings and structures at all. That is because they are always negotiable. Looking at Jesus' ministry it was the mes-

sage that was inflexible—'repent, the kingdom of God is near'—but the methods and approaches changed to suit the situation: two by two into the cities, parables and teaching for the crowds, actions and miracles with individuals. Perhaps young people and children need to be given more freedom to experiment with new forms for their situation. That is not to suggest that there are no lessons to be learnt, or nothing good to be retained, from previous generations. However, that inheritance should be imbued with new life from the next generation.

In *Telling the Story* Andrew Walker analyses changes in society and the relevant communication of the Christian faith. His conclusion that we will have to return to the ways of the monastery, community and sect is not to decry our more recent heritage, but points toward how the church might continue to fulfil its mission to be both the sign of the gospel and God's agent in mission for the next generation. The limiting factor over which most of us have control is the extent of our courage and imagination. The challenge is there again for those working with children or young people to allow new structures and forms to develop to express the age-old story for this generation.

Taking the Plunge

1.   What are the key features of the new relationship between people in the church? (Look at Ephesians 2:13, 15–16, 18, 19–22.) How credible do the following make the gospel: (a) your own relationships, (b) your youth and children's ministry, (c) your church fellowship?

2.   What would best describe the position of the children and young people with whom you work in relation to the local church: foreigners, strangers, fellow-citizens, or family members?

3.   How does Paul apply his statement about the church being a body (Romans 12:4) into the relationships and activities of Christians? (Look at verses 5 and following.) How many of these 'organic' features are present in your church?

4.   Look closely at 1 Peter 2:9–12 and note down the differences between what we 'were' and what we 'are'. Do you think the writer is suggesting complete separation between the Christian and non-Christian communities? (Look at verse 12 and following.)

5.   What do you think Jesus is referring to in John 6:53? What, according to verses 47 and 54, is the way in which eternal life may be found? How do, and should, the sacraments of the church (however your tradition defines and regulates them) be used in your work with children or young people?

6.   How does it make you feel to know that church structures and forms are largely negotiable? How can you respond to that challenge in the way in which your own work and ministry are structured?

Soaking In

If you thought that the only good things to come out of Sweden were Ikea and saunas, think again! The Swedish group study method is a great way to explore a Bible passage. Why not try it with Ephesians 2? You will need a piece of paper divided up into four sections. In the corner of each section draw one of the following (it does not matter what goes where): an arrow pointing down the page, an arrow pointing up the page, a candle with a flame and a question mark. Read through the passage and, as you do so, use your paper to jot down your ideas: questions next to the question mark; anything about God with the 'up' arrow; comments about human beings with the 'down' arrow; anything startling with the candle. You should now have a sheet of paper that gives you some idea about what the passage means and the questions it has raised for you. It would be good to take your questions and talk them over with your minister, other leaders or a knowledgeable friend. Alternatively, try looking in a good concordance, commentary (the IVP 'Bible Speaks Today' series or SU's 'Word for Today' are helpful), or Bible dictionary.

Overflow

Here are two activities to help you think about how your work relates to the local church.

• *Arrange to visit someone else's youth and children's work that is broadly similar to yours (i.e. church-based Sunday work, detached project, youth club, interest group-based, etc.). Take note of its strengths and weaknesses. If they do anything similar to you, how does it differ and why? Ask them what they feel is good and bad, where they struggle or succeed. You may find it helpful to hold in your mind the six images of church that this* Oasis *has looked at and think about how they relate to this situation.*

• *Ask a non-Christian friend to come to your group and record their impressions. Make it clear that you are not trying to convert them but are genuinely interested in what they think, and assure them that you will still be friends afterwards! Their observations may well provide you with a different but useful perspective as to what your work and church are really like and give some pointers about how the two can better relate.*

Flooded Out!

Doing an evaluation of your ministry gives an opportunity to address both specific issues, such as how the work relates to the adult church, and also its wider shape and direction. The basis of the evaluation could be your current activities, the six images of church in this *Oasis*, or a particular issue. If the results of an evaluation are to be useful they must be 'owned' by all, so make sure there is genuine involvement from the church, those leaders who are involved, and from the children or young people themselves. Those experienced in running evaluations make two important points:

• *Give it time. The most useful results come after thoughtful consideration.*

• *Ask all the difficult and awkward questions in a constructive spirit.*

• *Use an outsider, or agency (Diocesan or regional youth/children's staff, CPAS, Crusaders etc.), with good listening and observation skills. You are the experts in your own work, but another perspective can be very helpful. This can be enhanced if they are involved in youth and children's ministry, but it is not essential.*

A well-defined and focused evaluation, followed through by all, can refresh and renew both your own and the church's vision for youth and children's ministry, empowering both to carry things forward.

Plugging In...

Society at large

It's 4 o'clock and you can already hear the noise outside the door. As you open it, what seems like a whole heap of loud, frantic, messy children pile in, each making a beeline for their favourite activity. The table with the ingredients for peanut butter and banana sandwiches now swarms with little people. What was on the table is rapidly transferred to the floor, walls, clothes, faces and, occasionally, the bread. The afternoon outside looks grey. It always amazes you how different the estate feels depending on the weather. In the summer it can almost seem like a nice place to live in. But now, in late October, the dark clouds roll in, the rain sheets down and the concrete becomes dull and menacing. What little grass there is reverts to sticky mud. Standing in the doorway you can see small groups of children making their way to the hall across the rough ground. As they pass by concrete slabs with names like 'Sunnyside Mansions' and 'Hillview Towers', you wonder if the planners have ever visited the place since it dropped out the back of a cement mixer in the sixties. Turning away, your eye catches Tommy, a small lad who looks up at you with his broad mischievous grin. You know only too well that the face hides a complex and sometimes devious personality. Your eyes follow him into the room. But somehow it helps and you know that this small project, sacrificially supported by a struggling church on an anonymous, inhuman estate, does actually make a difference. You don't quite know how or why, but as time goes on and people ask why the church is bothering, there seem more and more opportunities to act and talk like Jesus.

For many people, youth and children's ministry is about small groups, teaching, Bible stories and Sunday mornings. These things are good. But we are called into a wider ministry than simply Sunday mornings, set within a society where God is interested in the whole, not just part. Throughout history God's people have functioned not just as evangelists and teachers, but also as prophets and leaders in society. Whilst some may prefer these two spheres of activity to be kept separate, the faith of the Bible and much subsequent Christian tradition keeps them together. It is not a case of 'either/or' when it comes to evangelism and social action, but 'both/and'. So we will take some time in this *Oasis* to consider society as another context within which youth and children's ministry takes place, and that affects the work of those in leadership.

Testing the Water

✴ Givers of salt   Matthew 5:11–16

You are like salt for the whole human race... (Matthew 5:13)

To try to improve society is not worldliness but love. To wash your hands of society is not love but worldliness.
    F. Catherwood, *Is Revolution Change?*

In an age of refrigerators and freezer cabinets the image of salt may well be lost on our modern ears. Salt is now merely a way of enhancing the flavour of our food. But salt also prevents decay. And in Jesus' day there was yet another fact about salt, which is followed through in verse 13. If salt loses its saltiness, then it has become worthless, so is thrown out. The salt from around the Dead Sea had just such properties, becoming less salty as the sodium chloride dissolved. This is in sharp contrast to sea salt, which retains its distinctive qualities. So the meaning becomes clearer. The way to keep on being salt for the whole human race is to remain distinct, through the life-giving waters of the Spirit. In a pluralist society with many different ideas, religions, and situations, perhaps the way forward for Christians is not to be found in becoming a mish-mash of every other good idea and philosophy that is around, but in actually affirming our distinctiveness. There is a difference between understanding what the world says so that we properly engage with it in communication and action, and taking on what the world believes so that we lose our distinctiveness, our saltiness. So for youth and children's leadership to engage with the social situation around us is not to let go of our distinctive beliefs and faiths. Rather it is to offer through them a holistic answer to the problems that face our world. Those in leadership are called to be givers of salt, active in making both their lives and ministries agents of both distinctive flavour and prevention of decay. In doing so we ourselves will benefit from all that God does through us.

✴ Lighters of lamps   Matthew 5:11–16

You are like light for the whole world... (Matthew 5:14)

He has asked us not merely to reflect it, but to be it.

Hulbert van Zeller, *Considerations*

There is no point in being light if you are going to hide yourself away—its whole purpose is thwarted. Light brings a distinctive change to its environment, bringing illumination and guidance. In calling the disciples 'light', Jesus is transferring to them a status and function that he also assigned to himself. Just as, in the Lord's prayer, Jesus invites us to relate to God as 'our Father'—taking on the distinctive term that he used about his own relationship to God—so here Jesus, 'the light of the world', has transferred to those who follow him that same property and function. So the light is not something we have to work hard at conjuring up, but the light of God within us that shines out to others. Such light must shine in order that, through our good deeds, 'people will praise your Father in heaven'. Again, our action and our beliefs need to be proclaimed simultaneously.

Perhaps the almost singular concentration on Sunday teaching that has characterized so much youth and children's work in our country for so long has actually become like salt that has lost its saltiness or light hidden under a bowl. Perhaps we need reminding that it did not start out this way: in the 1850s Robert Raikes initiated the Sunday school movement to teach reading and writing to the illiterate children of the workhouse, but did so using the texts of the Bible. The 'spiritual' and the 'social' were kept close together. Although with hindsight we can criticize the strong element of social control and patronization, there was an element of godly distinctiveness that is so often missing today. We need to rethink our ministry to reclaim the heritage of godly distinctiveness of being salt and light.

✳ Prophets of truth   Amos 3—5

When a lion roars, who can avoid being afraid? When the sovereign Lord speaks, who can avoid proclaiming his message?
   ... You people hate anyone who challenges injustice and speaks the whole truth in court. You have oppressed the poor and robbed them of their grain... Make it your aim to do what is right, not what is evil, so that you may live.
   (Amos 3:8; 5:10–14)

The gospel gives us different priorities from those of the popular cultures and offers us a different agenda from that of the political economy.

J. Wallis, *Agenda for a Biblical People*

Long hair and a beard? Or perhaps, sackcloth shirts, locusts and small jars of honey? Maybe lots of banknotes in a suitcase? Then again, possibly dark suits, big black Bibles and street corners? I wonder what comes into your mind when you think about prophets? (Note it's *phe* not *fi*!) It's probably true to say that prophets have suffered from an image problem. But whatever we may think of their dress sense, the prophets were revered in Israel and played a key role in both calling the nation back to

God and heralding the arrival of God's final solution in Jesus. And that brings us to Amos. We don't know what he wore, but we do know that he was not a professional prophet, paid by the state, but looked after sheep and fig trees. For the northern kingdom 750BC was relatively prosperous. Political alliances and relative social stability made it a good time for the nation, before the slide towards its two-stage annihilation in 589BC. But Amos could see the social injustices that signalled political and moral compromise: a lust for economic power, public revelling in luxury and indulgence, and, as we can see in chapter 5, the perversion of the law to suit the ruling classes.

The same biblical priorities, for the poor, the widows and the dispossessed—as David Sheppard coined, 'a bias to the poor'—are still Jesus' priorities. Christians are still called to operate in the sphere of the prophetic, of speaking God's truth into the structures, because, as Jim Wallis points out, our priorities and agenda are different. As leaders and ministers serving children and young people, we have a prophetic role, not in proposing good ideas to brighten their lives, but in proclaiming the priorities of God into the church and society as they affect them. And when the lion roars, who can fail but be afraid?

✳ Sharers of friendship   Luke 4:16—30

The Spirit of the Lord is upon me, because he has chosen me to bring good news to the poor. He has sent me to proclaim liberty to the captives and recovery of sight to the blind... (Luke 4:18)

Diaries are great when you're young. In fact you saved my sanity a hundred, thousand, million times... for you are my dearest friend and I shall thank you always for sharing my tears and heartaches and my struggles and strifes, and my joys and happiness. It's all been good in its own special way, I guess. See ya.

Anonymous, *Go Ask Alice*

The anonymous teenage author of the diary above died of an overdose three weeks after that, the last entry, dated 21 September. She was an ordinary, white, middle-class fifteen-year-old, but one who fell out of respectable society, into drug addiction and the world it opened to her. Even though she was in touch with her parents and living in, and out of, home right to the end of her life she fell out of society, and eventually out of life itself. And at the end of it all it is her diary which turns out to be her best friend.

The manifesto that Jesus read out at the start of his public ministry is a proclamation of God's saving friendship to all people. Given that Jesus talked both about the materially poor and about the spiritually poor, these words may well refer to both physical and spiritual realities. The ministry into which we are called to follow Jesus is one which proclaims and offers good news, liberty, healing and salvation through word and action. 'Alice' understood that people loved her, but somehow the reality of that love eluded her and she ended up believing the lies of her society. Her encounters with adults made her feel like she was 'garbage thrown in a disposal'. At one of the turning-points in her story it is an old priest who 'really understands young people' who negotiates a return home. We are not told why or how he 'understands', just that he does. It seems that he understood something of what it means to be a minister of Jesus. It is the willingness to follow Jesus in his identification and radical commitment to those on the edge, visible or invisible, of society that is such a challenge to youth and children's ministry today. It's part of the calling of ministry to do so: loving, listening, not judging—to take on our role as Jesus' hands, feet, eyes, ears, and mouth; the very substitute for his presence.

'Alice' was an ordinary, white, middle-class fifteen-year-old. You may have an 'Alice' now, amongst those with whom you work.

✳ Listeners who speak   Acts 17:16–34

That which you worship, then, even though you do not know it, is what I now proclaim to you. (Acts 17:23)

Listen! Do you want to know a secret? (Or should it be the other way round?) Someone is speaking amidst the noise, but the static makes it hard to hear. A certain amount of time must be spent in tuning the station.

M. Riddell, *alt.spirit@metro.m3*

I listened to a sermon the other day. It was a tough one. I could not put my finger on exactly what was wrong until I saw what was blindingly obvious. The speaker was on a completely different wavelength! Almost everything he said shot safely out of his mouth, flew gracefully through the air above my head and impacted just above where 'John Pugbladder lyeth'. Unfortunately the speaker was not 'tuning in the station', and those of us listening just heard noise.

In Acts 17 we find another sermon. Here the speaker tunes into the culture and society at large. Paul's message struck home to the Athenians because he was on their wavelength, 'for as I walked through your city and looked at the places where you worship, I found an altar'. He was then able to engage with their beliefs and situation, referring not only to their architecture, but also to their culture (look at verse 29). In order to speak and act distinctively in a culture you need to know what is distinctive about that culture. As well as giving attention to individuals, we need to give attention to the beliefs and structures of our society as a whole. Is your ministry tuned into one outdated station, listened to by a dwindling minority of young people and children? The result of tuning in is that people can hear, and if they can hear they can understand. If they can understand they can respond, and if they respond there is rejoicing in heaven. If you're tuned in you'll meet them again one day, Dionysis and Damaris.

✳ Fools who teach   1 Corinthians 1:18–31

God purposely chose what the world considers nonsense in order to shame the wise, and he chose what the world considers weak in order to shame the powerful. (1 Corinthians 1:27)

Perhaps the mission of those who love mankind is to make people laugh at the truth, to make truth laugh, because the only truth lies in learning to free ourselves from insane passion for the truth.

U. Eco, *The Name of the Rose*

Have you ever thought of yourself as a fool? What about those forty-inch purple flares in your wardrobe, bought because they were 'definitely you'? Or looking out on to the road, as I did for three years, and proudly surveying your new Austin Allegro Equipe: two doors, silver paint·job, go-faster stripes but sadly underpowered and built like a tank—I was once passed by a lady carrying her shopping! Being a fool doesn't feel too good; it's embarrassing, it attracts ridicule. But being a fool is an essential weapon in your pastoral armoury. Especially being a fool in relation to the society in which we live. Paul is clear when talking to the Corinthians that the message we have will seem like foolishness to those who look for philosophical wisdom or powerful signs. Likewise our words and actions will seem like foolishness to those who focus on themselves and seek to build their own kingdom. But every society needs its fools. For it is the fool who pricks the self-inflated pomposity of those in power, revealing their true motives and intentions. It is the fool who can poke fun at the attitudes and actions of a society that takes itself too seriously. It is the fool who can bring the truth to bear with pinpoint accuracy as society lets down its guard, considering such a person harmless. But as fools offering foolishness we are actually dealing in the wisdom and truth of God. In taking the role of the godly, guileless fool, we find that it is God's way of bringing holiness and freedom. For 'by him we are put right with God; we become God's holy people and are set free'. I suspect the day of the evangelistic Austin Allegro Equipe is some way off, but sometimes we need to laugh at, with, and in the truth to discover the freedom in God to which such truth points.

Taking the Plunge

1. In your work with children or young people, what elements of Christianity are particularly distinctive in relation to their culture?

2. What is the dual purpose of being 'like a light for the whole world'? (Look at Matthew 5:15 and 16.) What is the immediate context of Jesus' comments about salt and light? (Look at verses 11 and 12.) What might this teach us about the implications of seeking to obey his commands?

3. Review again the things against which Amos declares God's judgment. (Look at Amos 4:1, 5:10–13, 5:21–24, 6:8, 8:4–6.) Why do you think God declares these things to be wrong? (Look at 3:1–2.) How do the demands of Amos impact the way in which society treats your children or young people? (Look at 5:14–15, 23.)

4. Do you think Jesus' words in Luke 4:16–21 refer to the present or the future? Did Jesus come to bring judgment on people?

5. In what ways did Paul listen to, and use, the culture in which he found himself? (Look at Acts 17:16–18, 22–23, 28.) As you listen to the culture of your children or young people, what assumptions about God, the world, or people can you discern?

6. What is it about Christianity that Paul considers foolish? (Look at 1 Corinthians 1:18, 21–22.) In what ways might God be calling you and your ministry into foolishness?

Soaking In

Thinking about the state of our own society, the pain of broken relationships, the injustice and stigma of unemployment, the hopelessness felt by many, it can be difficult to know where to start, being a prophet, friend, or fool. It is at this point that we must return to the cross. As well as bringing salvation, the cross is also God's ultimate identification with a sinful and suffering world. It is only when we begin to see again the reality of a God who is 'Emmanuel—God with us', made fully concrete in the cross of Christ, that being salt, light, friend and prophet, listener and fool, becomes possible.

Take time to read John 19:16–42, slowly; it is the account of Jesus' crucifixion and death. As you do so try to imagine what he went through: the pain of carrying the cross; the sound of the hammer knocking blunt, iron nails through wrists and ankles; the abuse of the crowds and soldiers. God was willing to allow himself to be subjected to all this in an act of ultimate identification with and redemption of all his creation. Allow your mind to consider some of the issues facing the lives of the children or young people with whom you work. It is the suffering God who has relevance to them. Edward Shillito's poem, 'Jesus of the Scars', written after first-hand experience of the First World War, may be a helpful prayer.

> *The other gods were strong; but thou wast weak;*
> *They rode, but thou didst stumble to a throne;*
> *But to our wounds only God's wounds can speak,*
> *And not a god has wounds, but thou alone.*

Overflow

Arrange a time when your young people can respond to a set of questions, allowing the discussion to be led by them. Ask questions which get them talking about their world: What is your greatest fear? Who do you respect most? What is good about living in this country? Try to make sure the questions are open-ended and don't require 'yes' or 'no' answers. It would be an excellent opportunity to get them to bring along a friend. If you work with children you might want to encourage your children to draw picture on a particular theme: 'life today', 'my family', 'our world'. Each one may provide a good starting point for a discussion. Again it is important to let them set the agenda; what may seem random to us may be very significant. This activity may well generate ideas for the future direction of your ministry.

Flooded Out!

At your next leaders' meeting obtain a map of your local area. The aim of the exercise is to identify the sort of place in which you live, where your children/young people come from, what are their concerns, etc. It would be good to invite some of your members along as their input will be important. As you gather round the map, start by identifying where your members come from—you could use the small adhesive circles available from stationery shops to do this. Talk about what these places are like and what the social situations are. Around the map have six pieces of paper, each one headed with one of the following: salt, light, prophecy, friendship, listening, foolishness. Either all together, or in groups, aim to identify and write down issues that are relevant to your group, corresponding to each sheet of paper. Value and listen carefully to any members that you have invited. As a result of such an exercise you may decide that you need to go and walk round some of the places marked, pray more as a group, visit members from time to time, or even stop what you are doing and radically reassess your priorities, activities and style of work!

OASIS 10

Plugging In...

Give or take?

What would your workmates think if they could see you now? Sitting in a large pink (with blue dots) teacup, revolving at quite a speed, surrounded by six screaming seven-year-old girls! As the oversized crockery spins round for another stomach-wrenching turn, you wonder if a day out at the fun-park was really such a good idea. You rather fancied the family farm, but the group had different ideas. At last the spinning stops—truly there must be a God. The girls are chattering excitedly about what they want to do next. Whilst some of them head for the man selling abnormally large candyfloss, you wait next to the log flume with Sally, watching as the cars career down the final, soaking slide.

'Why,' asks Sally, 'is water wet? I mean, what makes it wet and not dry?'

It takes a few seconds for the question to sink in. And another few for you to realize that you haven't got a clue.

'Well,' you hesitate, 'it's because… err… well… err… because it's wet, rather it's liquid, isn't it? And liquid is what we call something when it isn't dry.'

'Oh, I see,' replies Sally in a tone of voice that implies she knows you haven't got a clue. Thankfully, at that moment five noisy children arrive back and you all troop off to the sky-ride. Later the same afternoon Sally comes up to you again.

'I've been thinking,' she announces as you begin to sweat nervously. 'You know you were talking about God's Spirit last week?'

'Yes…' you reply, cautiously.

'Well, when Mummy had Jake, my brother, she said that he had been living inside her and had to come out. That must be like God's Spirit who comes inside of us. And I suppose that we have to do things that show him coming out of us, like Mummy did to let Jake out. [Profound pause…] I hope that I can do things to let God's Spirit come out of me.'

You're not quite sure how to react, but find yourself smiling and saying, 'Yes, err… yes… err, well, I think you've got it right.'

'Anyway,' interrupts Sally, 'I thought the sky-ride was the best thing today.'

One of the things that you soon learn working with children or young people is that things do not always turn out as expected:

75

questions seem to come from nowhere or the best-planned talk falls on deaf ears. In this context leadership becomes a two-way process, one of both give and take. There are times when it is necessary, and right, to exercise considerable authority and direction and there are times when it is right to hang back and let those who are being led take the lead. In this *Oasis* we will consider some of these aspects of giving and receiving and, I hope, will begin to see that in God's economy the two are subtly linked as agents of mutual refreshment and blessing.

Testing the Water

✳ Come and see   Psalm 46

Come and see what the Lord has done. See what amazing things he has done on earth. (Psalm 46:8)

Step out of the traffic! Take a long, loving look at me, your High God, above politics, above everything.

Psalm 46:8, *The Message—Psalms*

A few years ago I had a job where I had to use the M25 at least three times each week. I would be guaranteed to end up stationary in what has been dubbed 'the biggest car park in England.' At times like that I would have given anything to have been able to 'step out of the traffic', to gain a bird's-eye view of exactly what was going on. And it is such an opportunity that Psalm 46 affords us. It gives us a vision of a God who is greater than us, our ministry, the church and even nature and the nations. Notice that the hardship does not disappear because we have faith; it is simply that we know where to go to find reliable shelter in such situations. As such, Christianity is not 'pie-in-the-sky' escapism from the rigours of everyday existence, but rather it is hard-nosed reality. Christians live in the real world, knowing that trouble will come, but

trusting that they have a shelter and a strength equal to the task. But God's power is so much more than simply a negative struggle against nature and life. The image of the city here, so prevalent throughout scripture, is one of strength and permanence. God's refuge is one that is high and uplifted, one that cannot be moved. The promise of peace is founded upon God's character and also upon his situation: in all senses he is a shelter and strength. There are times in ministry when the opposite seems to be the case. But so often God moves and works unexpectedly, perhaps because he can see the whole picture. So come and see what he has done in the past, believe his promise for the future and you will begin to appreciate something of the possibilities for his work in the present.

✳ Beyond the walls   Isaiah 45:1–19

'I myself have stirred Cyrus to action to fulfil my purpose and put things right. I will straighten every road that he travels … No one has hired him or bribed him to do this.' The Lord Almighty has spoken. (Isaiah 45:13)

There is no particle of creation and no experience of your in which he [God] is not with you.

G. Hughes, *God of Surprises*

It was a Sunday afternoon, the youth group had felt the need for a 'fag break', having coped with half an hour of abstinence, and we were laughing and joking in the late summer sun. As we talked about church it became clear to me that their antipathy toward the church certainly did not extend to God. In fact, someone who had come along for the first time talked about God, what he might be like and how he related to the world. In a tough urban area, talking to a teenage lad who had no contact with the church or Christian people, I was hearing words about God which, although wrapped up in his culture and language, were evidence of thought and questioning taking place.

I learnt an important lesson that afternoon, that God not only works on a wider scale than the church, but that he is actively involved in the lives of non-Christian people long before the church ever gets near them. In fact he seems to be quite happy choosing those who we might believe to be last on the list of people who

hear from God. Cyrus would not have been top of the list of Israel's allies, or followers of Yahweh. He was an all-conquering hero who ruled Babylon. However, the writer here makes clear that his actions resulted in the restoration of God's people, to God's place, at God's time. Whether by prediction, or from hindsight, the writer has seen that God works and uses people outside to bring about his purposes. An unlikely source of blessing for sure, but still Cyrus was God's chosen agent to bring blessing to his people.

Much ministry concentrates on those who are in the fold, within the walls, rarely looking beyond to where God might be working. To meet, serve and engage with children and young people who would not call themselves Christian may well be to discover God at work. In going beyond the walls we discover that it is not just so that we might give to those in need spiritually or physically, but also that we might receive from those in whom God is starting to do the impossible.

✳ Beyond just deserts   Job 42

After the Lord had finished speaking to Job, he said to Eliphaz, 'I am angry with you and your two friends, because you did not speak the truth about me, as my servant Job did.' (Job 42:7)

In the experience of God's living presence, Job discovers that human concepts of justice and the conclusions drawn by the human mind about God completely miss God.

A. Vogel, *God, Prayer and Healing*

What is it about other people's grass? It's always greener, lusher, thicker, and better cared for than mine. The grass is certainly greener on the other side of our fence. What is it about other people's ministries? They always seem to be better, more organized and attract more people than mine. Although we perhaps know better, many of us in ministry allow ourselves to think like

this too often. It is then that we need to go back to the Bible and have a think about Job. Job is often presented as some otherworldly paragon of virtue, the ever-patient, all-suffering spiritual superhero. Well there is another side to his story. Facing the loss of home, family, business and a threat to his own life, Job rails against God in furious, sarcastic, questioning anger, demanding an answer to his dilemma. Whilst the immediate circumstances are those of innocent suffering, the book of Job is also written on a larger canvas. At its heart is the issue of faith: what does it mean to have faith in God when all the odds are against you? Why does Job trust God? What does it mean to have faith when your life ministry seems to be falling apart, you have no leaders, the kids are half-hearted, whilst up the road, or across town, there is the mega-ministry, all leadered-up and ready for anything?

As God speaks to Job at the end of the book he does not give any easy answers, but talks of both priorities and reality. He seems to acknowledge the facile nature of a simplistic understanding of the ancient idea of just deserts (technically, divine retribution): if things go well, God is with you and you are good; if things go badly, God is against you and you must have done something bad. He affirms Job's emotional openness and reality. To claim that there is a place where we cannot know God or where we have completely failed him is to deny the depth and reality of God himself. To be able to receive from him in the midst of every situation is to refuse to acknowledge human ideas of justice and success in order to remain faithful to the unchanging and unending God.

Beyond the work   Colossians 2:4–10

Since you have accepted Christ Jesus as Lord, live in union with him. Keep your roots deep in him, build your lives on him, and become stronger in your faith as you were taught. And be filled with thanksgiving. (Colossians 2:6–7)

You are unlikely to have the power to be on the Godward side of human situations if you think that it can be done by a kind of shallow secularized activism.

M. Ramsey, *The Christian Priest Today*

'Shallow secularized activism' would be an apt description of some ministry amongst children and young people. If only we could do more, if only we could staff more activities and relationships, if only we could apply the latest technique or resource, our problems would be solved. Pursuing the 'if onlys' consumes leaders' time and energy and so public worship becomes an add-on extra, if time allows. Whilst such activity may be impressive on the surface, something rather different is actually happening. It is like a reservoir that has had its feeder rivers diverted elsewhere during a time of peak demand. The water level gradually lowers and lowers until it is unable to satisfy the demand. What water is left becomes stale and unfit for use. In writing to the Colossians, Paul knew that they were facing the temptation to look towards teaching and ideas other than true Christianity. His advice was to put their roots deep down into God, and to continue to do so. Then they would continue to be strong and effective, not a weak imitation of what they once were. Many youth or children's leaders need to rediscover this balance. Mature leaders will make sure that they put receiving as a high priority. It might be through tapes, midweek meetings or through Sunday services. Whichever it is, ministers must take in fresh and life-giving water on a regular basis. For those who have received have really got something to give: they have strength and purpose and are a true reflection of the message, not a weak imitation.

Beyond expectation   Philemon 1–7

Your love, dear brother, has brought me great joy and much encouragement! You have cheered the hearts of all God's people. (Philemon 7)

Children naturally learn how to do things by imitation, including prayer ministry (and any other ministry for that matter!) We are training them in ministry.

A. Price, *Children in Renewal*

In his letters, Paul almost always starts by telling the recipients something that they have shown or taught him, giving thanks to God because of it. The comments we find at the start of Philemon show again his openness to learn and be thankful for what God has given to him through others. In many ways these people were all his spiritual children, but Paul treated them as equals, each with something to give and contribute to himself and the wider church. In our ministry, do we come to meetings, streetwork, holiday clubs, residential activities, all with a sense of what God is doing? How often do we look for what God is teaching us through a par-

ticular individual? It is in giving time and attention to these things that ministry and faith grow stronger. Expectation is an important tool for building faith in those whom we serve and also in our perception of what God is doing in each of their lives. As expectation and faith are built, so like Paul, we experience joy and encouragement as the seed we have sown comes full circle and we learn lessons through the life of another in fresh and new ways. For such expectation is not based on vanity or pious wish-fulfilment. Rather it is based on the living God who has promised to honour what we do in his name.

Beyond today   Deuteronomy 31:14–39

The Lord said to Moses, 'You haven't much longer to live. Call Joshua and bring him to the Tent, so that I may give him his instructions.' (Deuteronomy 31:14)

Having spent a career trying to understand and help young people, I am convinced that the one primary cause of the tragic self-destruction of so many of our youth is that they do not know the worth and satisfaction of living for something larger than themselves.

J. Howard, *In Touch 3*

Reading the book of Joshua it would be easy to presume that Joshua appeared out of thin air, that Moses just looked around and thought, 'Oh look. There goes that Joshua; he seems like a nice chap and the sort of fellow who could run the nation when I die. I think I'll appoint him to be my successor.' But actually the story was somewhat different. Joshua, son of Nun, turns up earlier in Exodus and can be seen in the accounts of Israel's early history. He

is depicted as having served under Moses in some difficult situations. He has learned what it means to lead people, to direct them in God's ways, and has learnt by example how to put faith into practice. So when Moses anoints him for the work of taking the people into the promised land, he is ready, fit and willing for the task. Moses, following God's word, encouraged and enabled the young man to become all that he could be. Likewise, youth and children's leaders would be wise to remember that as well as being the children of today's church, children and young people are all potential leaders for tomorrow's church. The way in which we model leadership for them will be shaping not only their *own* Christian character and discipleship, but also the shape and nature of the church of the future. Whatever you are doing with children and young people, you will be affecting and developing their leadership style and skills by your teaching and example. Perhaps we need to allow them to learn leadership young and in so doing enable them to experience 'living for something larger than themselves'.

Taking the Plunge

1.   In which parts of your ministry do you find it hard to believe that God is 'exalted' or in control? Is Psalm 46 unrealistic in its statements about God's help?

2.   What does Isaiah 45 claim that God will achieve through Cyrus? What stops you from going 'beyond the walls' in your ministry with children or young people?

3.   Is numerical success a sign that God is blessing your youth and children's ministry? Given that the 'truth' Job spoke included questioning (9:24), anger (10:18–22), sarcasm (compare 23:8–9 with Psalm 139:7–12), reality and honesty (10:1), what place do, and should, these things have in your relationship with God and in your ministry?

4.   What issues distract or deter you in your Christian growth and discipleship? What is Paul's advice to the Colossians in this situation? (Look at Colossians 2:6–7, 17; 3:2–4.)

5.   What aspects of Philemon's faith affected Paul? (Look at verses 1–7.) Can you see these in any of the children or young people with whom you work?

6.   What is the basis of Joshua's right to lead the people of God? (Look at Deuteronomy 31:1–8.) How do you discern and develop leadership skills and vocations in the children or young people with whom you work?

Soaking In

As you think about the phrases and words that Paul uses to describe what he has received from Philemon, think about your own life:

• *Who would you consider to be brothers and sisters in Christ?*
• *Who have been your friends and fellow workers?*
• *Who has been an example of 'faith in the Lord Jesus' to you?*
• *Who has brought you joy, encouragement and great cheer?*

One way in which you can focus your thoughts is to try to create a sort of spiritual family tree for yourself. At the bottom of a piece of paper write your own name, at the top of the paper write 'God' and draw a line between the two. Now think of the people who have influenced and helped you on your own walk with God. Those currently fulfilling that role can be put on as branches directly above you; the higher you go, the further back in your life the people were. Remember, don't read too much into this sort of exercise! It certainly is not the case that those nearer the top of the page are any closer to

God! By making everyone linked to the same line between you and God it simply shows that all this comes from God. Pray that everyone in your 'tree' would come to a 'deeper understanding of every blessing we have in our life in union with Christ'.

Overflow

This is really worth doing, so don't be put off by the time it appears to take. For this exercise you will need to mark out one month on a sheet of paper and put it in a place where you will remember to complete it each day. At the end of each day make a note of any activity that you would classify as being to do with your ministry, then try to assess the balance, from your perspective, of that time: giving, receiving or both. Also mark in any time that you spent in developing your own faith: in prayer, study, time alone with God, listening to tapes, meeting your spiritual director, teaching times, sermons, going on retreat, etc. At the end of a month have a look at what the balance has been. Add up the total time for input, output and anything that was both. Does your input balance your output?

Obviously you will need to remember that length of time doing something does not indicate how valuable it was, so beware. However, although this looks primarily at the formal periods of input and output it is still a useful indicator.

If you find that you need more input you could, depending on your situation, use a few more sessions from *Jump into the Jacuzzi*, set aside one session a week to pray, give more time to your family, mark out time in your diary that is just for you with no agenda at all, make going to an evening service a priority (if not at your own church, then somewhere else); or perhaps you need to stop doing too much and concentrate on a few things in depth?

Flooded Out!

At your next leaders' meeting write down a list of questions that are of mutual concern to you all, about society, your own lives, your work with children or young people. Anything that is particularly personal should be phrased in the third person. Narrow the list down to nine questions, three for each topic. Arrange for the list to be looked at by children or young people from each age group represented at the meeting. The only rules that apply are as follows.

• *Leaders may set up a situation where the groups look at these questions but they must not lead, interrupt, or influence the answers in anyway. It may be easier for responses to be anonymous.*

• *Each group must be encouraged to do their own thing. They will need to decide how to give their answers: written down, video, cassette tape, computer file, drawings etc. And they must be encouraged to be as honest as possible.*

Examine the responses at your next leaders' meeting:

• *What surprises, angers or saddens us about these responses?*

• *What does this tell us about how well we know our groups and their concerns?*

• *What can we learn for our own spiritual lives from these responses?*

• *What changes can we make to our work to enable those with whom we work to give as well as receive?*

OASIS II

Plugging In...

Servant or leader?

*It had been a really great session. Fifteen fourteen-year-old lads
had turned up, more than ever before. Five leaders, and a hard,
fast game of indoor footie had left everyone exhausted. At the
end of the match it was really exciting to see the leaders, ordinary
church people, talking to the lads in groups of twos and threes. Every goal, foul
and move was analysed whilst ribbing each other about whose team was going
to win this season. After about half an hour people drifted off and once again
you found yourself left with the entire hall to clear up and clean. Each of your
fellow leaders had reasons for needing to get away: entirely reasonable, but completely maddening. The lads had drifted off down the road, looking to stretch
their time away from home as much as possible. But at half past ten, with at
least half an hour's cleaning to do and a big work meeting at nine the next
morning, the excuses seemed less than reasonable. Just as you are putting the
brushes back, there is a knock at the door. Tim puts his head round the door.*

*'Err... Tina, I was wondering if like, err... you know, I might be able to have a
lift home? I've missed the last bus and it's at least half an hour to walk. Mum will
kill me if I'm in at eleven again.'*

*You know all the stuff about serving the kids, but at that moment all you want
is for your bed to arrive through the door and whisk you away. But, as usual, you
go. 'Go on, you fool,' you say, smiling, 'get in the car, I'll just be a minute.'*

'Ta!' He smiles as he disappears.

*It's gone twelve when you finally crash into bed. As you try to sleep you think
about the other leaders and why they don't seem to pull their weight. Is this really
what it means to be the servant of all?*

Christian ministry turns the image of being a strong, go-ahead leader, in charge of and
served by all, on its head. In contrast to what much of the world believes, we are invited
in to the activity of being a servant. That does not mean that strength, focus and deci-
siveness are irrelevant. But it is in being a servant that we discover the ability to give and
receive in the manner that God intended. So as we look at some aspects of being a servant in this *Oasis*, allow yourself to discover that, in serving God and others, we find the
tables turned once again to find that we in turn are served, not simply by others, but by

82

God himself. And thus service becomes an opportunity for renewal, restoration and refreshment.

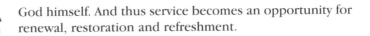

Testing the Water

✳ Served by God   John 13:1–20

So he rose from the table, took off his outer garment, and tied a towel round his waist. Then he poured some water into a basin and began to wash his disciples' feet and dry them with the towel round his waist. (John 13:4–5)

This is our God, the Servant King.

Graham Kendrick, *From Heaven You Came*

It is hard for us today to recapture the sense of sheer bewilderment and horror that must have gone round those first disciples as their master, their leader, their Lord, took the role of the menial slave and began to wash their feet. For the Jew, such a task was never done by peers; some thought that it was only fit for the lower orders of their society: Gentile slaves, women or children. Kneeling amongst the reclined diners at this, their last supper, he removed his outer garment and broke the silence, evidence perhaps of embarrassment and confusion over who was to perform this act for the group. In so doing he fulfilled his own statement that 'I come among you as one who serves' and yet another piece of the jigsaw surrounding his identity and mission slotted into place.

Most people still find it hard to allow someone else to serve them in the most intimate of ways. When I first started work I got a job as an auxiliary nurse in a care home. Part of my job as a young man was to help older people, including ladies, bathe, dress and look after themselves. It always amazed me that they were willing to let me do this for them and I had to learn that such a task was indeed a great honour. In our reserved English culture we avoid embarrassment and shun the attention that being served attracts. However, at the heart of the Christian faith is an incredible truth: it is the living God who serves us. Before it is possible to serve others in the name of God, Jesus makes it clear that we must allow God to serve us. Immediately we want to say, 'No, I'm not worthy, I must serve you.' But the fact is that God wants and has to serve us, symbolized by Jesus' initiative in washing his disciples' feet, where he takes his self-emptying life another step further towards the supreme act of service: crucifixion and death. In contrast to what we think, God not only loves us, he actually *likes* us, so to be made and redeemed in his image entails allowing, receiving and enjoying his ministry, his service, to us in which we become the centre of his lavish attention and love.

✳ Service and power   John 13:1–20

'...All of you are clean—all except one.' (Jesus already knew who was going to betray him; that was why he said, 'All of you, except one, are clean.') ... Judas

accepted the bread and went out at once. It was night. (John 13:10–11, 30)

> *To dress myself in humble cloth, and walk*
> *Without the sparkle of my cherished jewels*
> *Seems gray, a drab retreat, the path of fools:*
> *The diamonds of my friends, entice me, mock*
> *Such sterile ways…*

D. Carson, 'Fourteen'—Holy Sonnets of the Twentieth Century

Have you ever noticed how much power there is in the language and acts of service? Service can so easily be used in false modesty to try to shame others into the actions we want them to take. What is supposed to be a selfless activity actually becomes intensely selfish as we seek to manipulate others: the sarcastic tone as we begrudgingly do more than is necessary, the refusal to allow someone space to act in their own time. Jesus' example and illustration of service is also a powerful act, but one that could not be further from cynical manipulation. Because, in his service, power is systematically laid aside in favour of weakness. No doubt Judas, who had his feet washed, had been hoping for a political leader who would overthrow the Roman oppressor. He wanted a flashy display of power that would confirm the divine identity and activity of his Messiah.

But Jesus went another way, that of service and submission to God's will—the only course of action that could bring salvation for all people. The disciples, despite their impetuous nature and lack of understanding, were 'already clean'. Their faith had put them right with God and washed them spiritually clean, just as a bath washes a person physically clean. So the service into which we are called as ministers, in imitation of Jesus, is one where we lay aside our own power. In such an act the power of God may be seen, as others find that it is not simply us who serve them, but God who serves them through us. What may seem like the 'gray, drab retreat of fools', whilst the 'diamonds of friends entice', is actually a powerful activity that illustrates and effects the cleansing, saving service that God offers freely to all who respond.

✱ Service and cleansing   John 13:1–20

'If I do not wash your feet,' Jesus answered, 'you will no longer be my disciple.'
Simon Peter answered, 'Lord do not wash only my feet, then! Wash my hands
and my head, too!' Jesus said, 'Those who have had a bath are completely
clean and do not have to wash themselves, except for their feet. All of you are
clean—all except one.' (John 13:8–10)

The soul sees that… though he cannot save himself, Christ can. Though the fig-leaves
of our own unrighteousness are too short to cover our nakedness, the righteousness of
Christ is large enough.

R. Baxter, The Saints' Everlasting Rest

It soon becomes clear that Jesus is moving beyond simply showing moral behaviour, encouraging his disciples to be nice to each other. He is talking about another cleansing, a cleansing that is essential to being linked with him. We cannot tell

exactly how much Peter understood about Jesus' mission at this point. Reading through the gospels it is clear that the disciples had a patchy view of exactly who Jesus was and what he had come to achieve. Certainly they would have been poor members of any confirmation class or Alpha course! But Peter, exuberant as usual, gets hold of the basic idea and asks for a complete cleansing. If there's any blessing going from Jesus, Peter is certainly up for it! Thus the act of laying aside power and submitting to the washing of God is one of humility. Servant leadership is humble leadership because it has itself submitted to the cleansing that only God can offer. It is not the grovelling, cloying humility of Dickens' Uriah Heep, who is 'ever so 'umble' in the hope of personal return. It is the humility that has already seen the return. It is the joyful and devoted response of one who has a 'part with' Jesus because they have been washed by him. As Richard Baxter explained, it is only Christ who could save, and on that basis he would later encourage his people toward devotion and service of others. To serve others is to be a humble, living example to them of what they need to allow God to do for them.

✳ Service and suffering   John 13:1–20

Isaiah said this because he saw Jesus' glory and spoke about him ... I am telling you the truth: slaves are never greater than their master, and messengers are never greater than the one who sent them. (John 12:41, 13:16)

When a man bears patiently a number of heavy disasters, not because he does not feel them but because he has a high and generous nature, his nobility shines through.
Aristotle, *Ethics—Book One*

Aristotle would have made a good Englishman, or woman. Stiff upper lip, keeping going, queuing for the bus in the rain, whichever one you choose there has always been a certain type of English person for whom bearing things patiently has been refined to an art form. It's all good character-building stuff. We put up with things, we show the depth of our character by making do, not complaining, just getting on with it. But, whilst Aristotle may have had a point, it is not a Christian view. We do not suffer because we want our character to shine through, or because we enjoy courting disaster. We suffer because it is following in the footsteps of Jesus. It is interesting that John has Jesus placing himself as the supreme fulfilment of the suffering servant of Isaiah 53 immediately before his account of the last supper. Like the servant, Jesus caused astonishment, was rejected by the people and ultimately exalted by God himself. The suffering of Jesus and his followers is not a matter of self-abuse, denial, false modesty, or ascetic religion. It is the way of the cross and the very heart of Christianity; it is the way through which God has chosen to speak. As Paul wrote to the Philippians, we want to 'know Christ and experience the power of his resurrection, to share in his sufferings and become like him in his death' so that 'we ourselves will be raised from death to life'. It is this sharing in his sufferings as well as his resurrection that is what he has previously called the 'surpassing value of knowing Christ Jesus my Lord'. Early missionaries understood this. When they packed their belongings to go overseas they packed their coffins to go with them. Christian service meant that they would share in Christ's sufferings, even to death.

As we move to a missionary mindset in our youth and children's ministry, perhaps we too will discover the reality of Paul's phrase and in so doing recapture another facet of the 'surpassing value of knowing Jesus Christ as our Lord'. After all, 'slaves are never greater than their master, and messengers are never greater than the one who sent them.'

✳ Service, the servant and master

John 13:1–20

I am telling you the truth: whoever receives anyone I send receives me also; and whoever receives me receives him who sent me. (John 13:20)

God does not appear to use angels for this task [evangelism]... It is only pardoned sinners who can invite others to the cross of Christ. It is [only] an amazing privilege to be given such a sacred trust.

M. Green, *Evangelism through the Local Church*

I could never work out if I was being offered the bargain of the century or being conned completely. They always came to the door and knocked confidently, they were well turned out and had a compelling patter, but I could never quite work out what was going on. The problem with people selling door-to-door is that the whole exercise relies on their ability to persuade you of the quality or value of their goods. You cannot talk to the person who designed or made the item, or even someone who has used it. The sale depends on either the salesperson's ability to sell or, as in my case, the gullibility of the householder. I should have learned after the third set of cloths that fell apart! How often in ministry do we believe exactly the same thing? The response of these people depends on my powers of persuasion or my ability to love them. So we try very hard to get everything absolutely right, and so we should. We pray very hard that God will bless it, but when it comes down to actually getting on with it, I think most people believe that God is absent at some distance and will just keep an eye on us, perhaps helping out if things get too tricky. But Jesus here foreshadows his commission in chapter 20 and tells the disciples a stunning truth: that where they go he goes with them, and if he is with them then it is God himself who is being seen and received in the relationships they offer. The creator God who made the universe will be there, not at a distance, not three steps removed, but as they step out in service. As the servant serves, so the master is revealed and that is an incredible and amazing privilege of a truly sacred trust.

✳ Service as freedom   John 8:31–47

If the Son sets you free then you will be really free. (John 8:36)

> *O God, the author of peace*
> *and lover of concord,*
> *to know you is eternal life,*
> *to serve you is perfect freedom.*
> *Defend us your servants*
> *from all assaults of our enemies;*
> *that we may trust in your defence,*
> *and not fear the power of any adversaries;*
> *through Jesus Christ our Lord. Amen.*

The Second Collect, for Peace, *Alternative Service Book, 1980*

If it had been me, I would have laughed. In fact I would have screamed. In all honesty I might have kicked. You see, I hate having my feet touched, especially underneath.

But to have someone wash them, it would have been torture! I find that the sensation makes me laugh and if persisted with is painful. So it would have been quite a humorous time if I had been at the last supper and, in some ways, that would not have been too out of place, since the servant/master relationship into which Jesus calls us is fundamentally one of freedom.

In John 8, set in the context of a discussion about what brings freedom, the law or Jesus, and encouraging true discipleship, Jesus once again points to himself, rather than birth or position, as the source of God's blessing. Jesus sets us free from the effects of sin. We are not free from sin itself, but we are from its *effects* and as such, as the Anglican prayer book recognizes, his service is perfect freedom. Such freedom is a cause of rejoicing, and possibly even fun! It is easy when thinking of service to conjure up ideas of drudgery and slavery to an overbearing master whose demands are ridiculous. But the service into which we are called is that of freedom. That freedom enables us to be served and to serve Jesus. That freedom makes Christian service a subversive activity. Because as we serve, it is the eternal God who is working through all that we are and say. Growing as a servant leader will mean growing in our freedom to lay aside ourselves and joyfully follow our Lord into whatever ministry brings. That is not wishful thinking, or ignoring reality, it is taking hold of all that being the Lord's servant means, believing it and living it out in each new situation. And as the world sees servants who are free, then they will begin to see and experience Jesus himself at work. Because if he sets you free, you are free indeed!

Taking the Plunge

1. What sort of feelings do you think the disciples would have had as Jesus started to wash their feet? In what ways are we reluctant to let God serve us?
2. In what ways do you think Judas was disappointed by Jesus? What expectations do you have of Jesus? In your own ministry what sort of power do you have to lay aside in order to offer service?
3. Do you think Jesus means that people need to be cleansed once, or that such an act was needed more than once? How do you point people to the cleansing that God offers through your ministry?
4. What does your suffering, or lack of it, say about the nature of your following of Jesus' example in word and action?
5. Has there ever been a time when you know God has used you in his service? What was it like? Is it always a good thing to have people confronted with Jesus as we build relationships with them?
6. To whom was Jesus speaking in John 8:38? (Look at verse 31.) On what did they base their freedom? (Look at verse 33.) Is there any such equivalent in your situation today?

Soaking In

Try this two-person meditation with a friend or fellow leader. Start off by reading together John 13:1–20, slowly and carefully—one could read to the other, or both together, or one verse at a time. Try to imagine the scene again as you read. Now do what it says! Take some time to wash each other's feet to experience what it might have felt like. As you do so, talk about the experience, and don't be afraid to laugh! Try to think of three words that best describe the experience.

When you have finished look at John 13 and try to find verses or passages that best correspond to each of your words. Now pray together using your three passages and words. Pray them for each other, and for the rest of your church and team. Pray them for the young people or children as they mature. Finish your praying by asking God to serve and cleanse you afresh for his service. You might want to use the Collect for Peace as a way of finishing.

Overflow

This is an idea for you to do with your group that will enable you both to serve them and to build relationships with them. A few years ago there was a Saturday evening TV programme called 'Jim'll Fix It'. The presenter asked people to write in with a dream and some were set up for a few lucky people. Why not offer your group the chance of having a 'Fix It'. They can ask for anything they want and, if at all possible, you will fix it for them. One Christian holiday camp did this and arranged for children to stay in a hotel, and watch £1,000,000 being burnt at the Bank of Scotland (the bank does it once a week to dispose of worn-out notes!)—receiving a spontaneous standing ovation and a whole lot more. The activity speaks of your willingness to serve them, and also is an illustration of God's lavish and individual service and concern for them. It is worth making the effort, and if you are persistent the whole thing can be arranged through goodwill and requires little or no money. Make sure you go with each one to build relationships and take the photos!

Flooded Out!

Why not try to develop a culture of service within your team? For instance, you could pair them together to care for and look after each other, if they are not already linked into some other small group structure. You could make those pairs a substitute for being part of other groups to save on their time. Alternatively you could challenge your team from time to time to do acts of random kindness for one another. This is like a nice sort of terrorism. They do not have to reveal who has done it but the key is to do it unannounced, unexpectedly and with great joy: turn up with a ready-meal, do all their washing, send them free cinema tickets, take them out for a walk… whatever is most appropriate. Such things are often the start of an attitude that takes over the whole team and affects not only the leaders but those whom you seek to serve as they notice the difference.

Home and ministry

'Surely not again?' Your partner's face drops as you put on your coat. 'You can't have another meeting. You've been out every night this week. Sometimes I wonder if I'm still married, you're always going out.'

You wince inside, only too aware that the new outreach project to children has just got busier and busier. The worst thing is that you can predict the course of the discussion and you just don't have the energy to argue the whole thing out. It's not that you don't love your partner any more, it's just that your time has become taken over with this project. It's so exciting to see children coming along who have no other contact with Christian people. You thought that you were serving God, but it only seems to have ended up in this mess. As you search around for the car keys your mind searches for the right words to say.

'Look love, I'm sorry. I know things have got out of hand. We'll talk about it when I get back in; honest, we can work it out.'

'Yeah, I know, but I just wonder what is more important, your precious children or me. I thought the church was supposed to support marriages, not rip them apart.'

'Come on,' you retort, 'you know that's not fair. I know it's my fault, but you don't have to blame the church.'

'There you go again, defend it at all costs.'

Before anything else can be said, you head for the door. 'I'll see you later.'

'Yeah, yeah, yeah...' A jab at the remote control brings the TV noisily into life. Communication has ended for another evening.

As you pull the front door shut behind you, you wonder what it's like for everyone else. Are you the only couple this happens to?

The pressure of balancing home life and ministry is equally diffi-cult for single and married, for volunteer and full-time. The strong motivation behind youth and children's work, the near blackmail techniques of those in management, and the sense of calling and emotional commitment, although all fine in principle, can some-times conspire to the abuse of the worker, their friends and fami-ly, and ultimately the whole church. Such pain is also felt and expe-rienced by God himself. The family and household is meant to be a

89

foundation of the church, a place where faith is lived out day by day, a priority and, most of all, a place of joy where the grace of God can be found. In this *Oasis* we will be looking at some principles that may help protect these relationships. Although the issues are never simple these basic principles are explored in the belief that God cares passionately about each and every home situation. Whilst each must be explored with great sensitivity and discernment to different situations God can still bring relief, healing and refreshment into the hardest areas: with him it is possible for the deserts to flow with living water.

Testing the Water

✳ A place that shows grace
Ephesians 5:21—6:4

Submit yourselves to one another because of your reverence for Christ. (Ephesians 5:21)

*Family n. (pl. **ies**) 1 a set of parents and children, or of relations, living together or not.*

The Oxford Concise Dictionary, eighth edition

I wonder how you think of your family: a battleground, a celebration, a refuge? There are probably as many answers as there are people living in families. However, few people today can fail to have been touched by the pain and anguish of families going through difficult times. For many in ministry their own family is something that is separate from what they do within their Christian service. Some feel it is irrelevant, others see a clear separation between the two, and many struggle to keep it apart from their ministry.

But whilst we need to be sensitive to individual situations, the family is at the heart of the Christian community and faith. Undoubtedly the New Testament has in mind something more than simply mum, dad and two children. The Bible points to a wider community—a network of relationships centred around parents and children, in which responsibility and roles are shared and where people in, and out of, relationships can find a place of friendship and safety in a place where God's grace is experienced. Having outlined the nature of God's new community, the church, Paul applies his arguments to family life. Whilst sometimes misunderstood, Paul is making an important point: that the relationships between members of the family are to be an example of the grace of God. Women, men and children are to look to Jesus as their example of how they should behave towards each other. Whatever view one may take on headship (and other arguments) the context is one of shared service, one to another: at the sink, with the shopping, in times of fun, in all that goes to make up home life.

For those in ministry the same is true: the household in which we live is the primary place where we live out our love and service of Jesus. If the children and young people whom you serve could see your family life, would it be a place of grace?

✱ A priority for leaders   1 Timothy 5:8

If anyone does not take care of his relatives, especially the members of his own family, he has denied the faith and is worse than an unbeliever. (1 Timothy 5:8)

If it's Wednesday, this must be prayer meeting; if I'm home, you must be my wife!
Duffy Robbins, *Youth Ministry Nuts and Bolts*

Some of my close friends have grown up as 'PKs'—preacher's kids. As we have talked I have begun to understand just a little of what it is like for the children of 'full-time' Christians. But it is not only the children of full-time workers who find it hard. Anyone living in any household where there is service to God and his church has probably experienced the sense of the goldfish bowl, of unreal expectations, tensions of belief, overworked people and a whole host of other issues.

As Paul writes to Timothy, I think he has such pastoral concerns in mind. He knows that the family is to be a place and sign of God's grace, but equally he is a realist and knows that it takes time and effort. And so in giving advice about who should serve in the church as leaders, he makes a point of highlighting the sort of priorities that they should have, and as such they apply to all in Christian leadership. He is not suggesting that the home be used as an excuse for not getting involved in church, but rather saying that leaders who are involved should make it a priority, especially where it concerns

the care and protection of children. It is not about keeping up a good front, or living like the perfect 'cereal advert' family. It is about giving time and attention to relationships that should experience God's grace through loving service.

Elsewhere, when writing to Timothy, Paul has pointed out that he is looking for progress, not perfection. So when thinking through our responsibilities and actions it is vital to protect both our families and ourselves, in order to exercise healthy and holistic leadership. Homes and families don't build themselves and those that don't spend time building will fall quickly to disrepair and ruin. Whether it's a specific night set aside for family time, spending uninterrupted time with the children, building good relationships with flatmates, visiting parents or relatives, or spontaneous romantic acts for your partner, it is important. It's not in competition with your ministry, but it is what makes your ministry both possible and complete. In the midst of such progress God will be honoured and found, and ministry will be blessed.

✱ Mixed marriages?   1 Corinthians 7:12—16

For the unbelieving husband is made acceptable to God by being united to his wife, and the unbelieving wife is made acceptable to God by being united to her Christian husband. (1 Corinthians 7:14)

The 'sanctification' in mind is clearly not a transformation of character into the likeness of Christ. As John Murray puts it, 'the sanctification of which Paul speaks… must be the sanctification of privilege, connection and relationship.'
J. Stott, *Issues Facing Christians Today*

One of the often unspoken facts of life for many youth or children's leaders is that they have a partner who does not share

their faith. The ministry can become a focus of tension between the two parties. There is not time to explore this important subject in a great deal of depth, except to point out some of the positive things that Paul brings to the mind of the Corinthian church in the face of such issues of 'mixed' relationships. Firstly, he recognizes that they exist. One of the most destructive things that can happen is that the spouse becomes a hidden person. They are not mentioned to the children, other leaders or the church. They are kept to one side, dearly loved, but not acknowledged within the church context. Honesty and openness are vital for the health of all concerned.

Secondly, he recognizes that with God anything is possible; therefore partners should not split—their marriage is important to God and in his eyes should, if at all possible, be cherished and preserved. The way forward is not in aggressive personal evangelism, but in practical love and service. Paul is not saying, 'Marry a non-Christian, because you will convert them.' Rather, he is speaking to those who are already married. Don't split, unless there are genuine grounds in God's eyes, and look for God to work.

Finally, Paul recognizes that the people of God and the Christian faith are corporate, offering a place for all people. As John Stott explains, we don't know exactly what Paul meant by 'sanctification' ('made acceptable' in the Good News Bible) in this case, but the implication is clear: we are not to make people hidden embarrassments, but to welcome them honestly and lovingly as connected to and involved with the community of faith, lovingly supporting both leader and partner. Such relationships should not primarily be seen as an automatic cause of trouble and concern. Rather, with God, there is always the potential for blessing.

✳ Single issues?   1 Corinthians 7:32–35

…I want you to do what is right and proper, and to give yourselves completely to the Lord's service without any reservation. (1 Corinthians 7:35b)

The single life is a great gift, to be enjoyed and used to the full. Jesus and Paul taught this, the early Church understood and embraced it. It is a jewel—jagged and painful sometimes, but a jewel none the less—needing to be rediscovered by the Church, by individual Christians, and by society today.

A. Cornes, *Divorce and Remarriage—Biblical Principles and Pastoral Practice*

'Jagged' and 'painful' are within the experience of most single people in the church. In so many cases, churches and Christians have so valued and encouraged marriage that single people have often felt that they are second-class and inferior, that they are not whole people. It is assumed that the single state is actually a permanent waiting-room for marriage. It's incredible how easily newly-married couples can act insensitively toward others who do not share their particular joy. In addressing the relational problems that existed within the Corinthian church Paul deals, amongst others, with issues surrounding marriage and singleness, in chapter 7. A key point is made at the end of the section, that Paul wishes that people would 'give themselves' completely to the Lord's service 'without any reservation'. This is applied by pointing out some of the advantages to Christian people of the single calling. It may be that you are freer to make decisions to move, or how to spend your time, or resources.

This is not to say that single people must become the slaves of the church whilst those who are married sit around and do nothing! Nor is it to say that single people don't have families, or homes, for whom they share a responsibility. Or course all people are called to both serve God and exercise a responsibility to their family, married or single. So singleness, although not always sought and sometimes painful, should not be seen as a life sentence or sign of personal inadequacy. In contrast to the negative attitudes of the world towards singleness, for Christians it is a calling within which people may give and receive from others in a way that is not open to those with marital commitments. It is neither a greater or lesser calling than marriage; each person should make a decision for themselves. Whatever each decides, the key aim is to live a life pleasing to God. Your, or another leader's, singleness is actually a gift from God to you and your ministry, which all should honour, cherish and celebrate.

✳ Hospitality matters
Romans 12:13, Hebrews 13:2

Share your belongings with your needy fellow-Christians, and open your homes to strangers. (Romans 12:13)

We accept the distinction between necessities and luxuries, creative hobbies and empty status symbols, modesty and vanity, occasional celebrations and normal routine and between the service of God and slavery to fashion.

An Evangelical Commitment to a Simple Lifestyle,
Lausanne Occasional Papers, No.20, 1980

I could never quite work out what it was about the family to whom we used to go for home-group. There was something distinctive, a qualitative difference, but one that seemed somewhat elusive. In fact it took about a month to work it out. They were committed to a simple lifestyle. This was not a 'sackcloth and ashes' type of existence, but one where need was the guiding principle as to the use of finance and resources. The experience has stuck with me for a number of years and, even greater than the physical differences, there was a qualitative difference in the atmosphere of the home. Here was a place of simplicity and joy, but not in an escapist or naive sense.

As I look round my own possessions I am constantly challenged as to the place I give them and their true worth in God's eyes. The issue of simplicity in lifestyle and the offering of hospitality has gone down in the Church's agenda in recent years, but we need it more than ever before. How we choose to use our possessions and resources is a bit like a barometer of our spiritual health. If we really do trust God and see our material goods in the right perspective we will be joyful in sharing them with others. It was wisely said that when a man gets converted he does so in this order: 'mind first, right foot second (think about it!) and wallet last'. However useful the latest prayer technique, youth-group course or training activity is to our ministry perhaps the really significant changes lie closer to home: our generosity, hospitality and simplicity. As these things are sought and shared we begin to discover the blessing that God bestows on those willing to give.

✳ When to pull out   1 Timothy 3:1—7

For if a man does not know how to manage his own family, how can he take care of the church of God? (1 Timothy 3:5)

Our first responsibility is to the ministry God gives us with our families. Obviously, departure is the last resort, but any job responsibility that effectively prevents us from carrying out that ministry gives us grounds to resign from our posts.

Duffy Robbins, *Youth Ministry Nuts and Bolts*

At the end of this last *Oasis* it is time for something that does not fit entirely with the theme, but could not find its place anywhere else! Imagine the scene: it's the back of church and the vicar approaches you. After a fruitless attempt at hiding behind the bookstall you are cornered.

'Hi, how lovely to see you,' purrs the vicarial voice. You know in an instant that he wants you to do something. Before you can object you find yourself agreeing to run the under-threes group, 'just until someone with real skills comes along'. Five years later you're still there. For many youth or children's leaders there was no formal start to their ministry, and as such there is no agreed end-point. We just keep going out of guilt, or a desire not to disappoint. Alternatively, we burn out and give up suddenly with no follow-on leaders prepared. But we do not become a Christian to become a volunteer. We are called to worship God and that must come first. Whether you have done it for two or twenty years it is always wise to ask yourself, 'Should I still be doing this?' It may be that there are younger leaders who need

to be allowed to develop. God may have another job for you to do. It may be that you need a short break, that your time has naturally come to an end, or that you need to concentrate on home and family.

Whatever the situation, there is no scriptural rule that you must keep going regardless of circumstance. All the biblical characters we have come across in *Jump into the Jacuzzi* had to lay aside their ministries at some point, at different times and for different reasons. As Paul writes to Timothy he makes it clear that there are some circumstances when ministry should be left to one side. For some people the refreshing that God wants to bring is new waters, in a new place, in a new ministry. That is not to suggest that we should become inactive in the faith but simply that we learn to hear God's voice and, if it becomes clear that it is time to go, that we trust God, take hold of the future he has for us and move on in obedience and expectation. Stale water does no one any good, so perhaps it's time for something different?

Testing the Water

1. Read Ephesians 5:21—6:4. In what ways are husband and wife supposed to imitate Jesus in marriage? How can you see this in practice in the marriages you know? How can you help and support them?
2. How do you exercise your responsibilities to your household?
3. What may be some of the difficulties for those in 'mixed' ministry? (If you don't know, find someone and ask them.) Do you have a role in supporting someone, either Christian or non-Christian?

4. Do you think Paul's advice is realistic? Try to explain your answer.
5. To what extent do you try to practise (a) simplicity, (b) generosity and (c) hospitality? Is God calling you to a greater emphasis on any, or all, of these?
6. Why should you continue in your ministry?

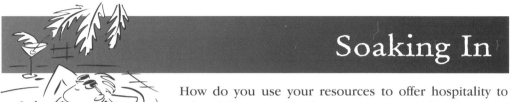

Soaking In

How do you use your resources to offer hospitality to others? Not everyone has vast amounts of money, or a large house, but the challenge is still there to put our faith into action by the way in which we welcome and care for others.

Why not look at how you spent your time last month, how much hospitality was offered? How did you use what resources you had available? It may be helpful if you have a bank account to look at the most recent statement and see what you actually do with what God has given to you.

I heard of someone who once a year takes a whole month's salary out in cash and puts it on a table to look at. It is a reminder of just how much he is given each month, and therefore how much is available to God. In what for many is a cashless age, we can easily underestimate the wealth that many enjoy.

Both of these exercises could be done during a meditation on Romans 12. Allow each verse to penetrate your mind and, as you look at the bank statement, or the money, think through the people you have met, the needs at church, the children and young people you serve. What would Paul have said to you about your hospitality towards those people? Do you need to give or receive? Remind yourself that God has given so much to each one of us in Jesus, and so we should willingly respond with thanks with what we have to offer.

Overflow

If you have been involved in ministry for three years or more, look ahead at your diary and plan a time when you can have a sabbatical! This might be a term off (probably the easiest) or, if you work the whole year through, pick a two-month stretch that is usually fairly quiet. You could get the young people or children with whom you work involved in helping you think about what you might do with the time: you could use the rest of this book, or plan some major project, or research some major issue. Basically allocate any time that you would have spent with children or young people to something else: the family, prayer, fly-fishing, listening to music, taking your spouse out, research etc… Liaise with your coordinator and try to use such a time to look at your future and your future ministry. If you work with older teenagers then why not leave the group in their hands and see what happens—you might be amazed. Whatever happens, make sure you get life back in balance through this and receive what God has on offer.

Flooded Out!

One way of supporting and protecting leaders in their ministry is to ensure that you make use of job descriptions. These need not be terribly formal documents, but they provide something firm against which discussions about length of service and future development can take place. Those who have used them suggest that the key is keeping them simple, clear and mutually agreed. Drawing them up with leaders will provide an ideal opportunity to look at where the work is going in the long term and make any necessary adjustments.

Decide on the length of service. Depending on your situation you could make this one or two years long. Make sure you set a date for review. At a minimum the job description should outline what is expected of the leader, and what they can expect by way of support, budget etc. If you have any written policies or vision statements these could be attached to the agreement. Most people find that their leaders begin to feel more secure and confident in what they are doing when they know what their parameters are. They also know they have an 'opt-out' clause! Devising job descriptions also helps long-term 'staff' planning and as such should contribute to a more stable and well-organized leadership team.